SAVE
BRITAIN'S HERITAGE
1975–2005
THIRTY YEARS OF CAMPAIGNING

MARCUS BINNEY

SAVE

BRITAIN'S HERITAGE

1975–2005

THIRTY YEARS OF CAMPAIGNING

S
C
A
L
A

DEVELOPMENT AND REGENERATION EXCELLENCE

SAVE Britain's Heritage 1975–2005

3 November 2005 – 12 February 2006

V&A + RIBA Architecture Gallery

Victoria and Albert Museum

This edition © copyright Scala Publishers Ltd 2005

Text © copyright Marcus Binney 2005

First published in 2005 by

Scala Publishers Ltd

Northburgh House

10 Northburgh Street

London EC1V 0AT

ISBN 1 85759 440 1

Editors: Oliver Craske and Sarah Peacock

Design: Misha Anikst and Alfonso Iacurci at Anikst Design

Production Director: Tim Clarke

Printed in Italy

10 9 8 7 6 5 4 3 2 1

Front cover: Holy Trinity Church, Rugby, under demolition. *The Rugby Advertiser*

Inside front flap: The Grange. *Marcus Binney.*

Inside back flap: The staircase hall, Tyntesfield. *James Mortimer*

Page 2: 18th-century state bed, Calke Abbey. *The National Trust*

Page 12: *Robin Wade*

Page 28r: *New Society*

Catalogue Illustrations

All images are courtesy of **SAVE** Britain's Heritage except as follows:
1: Dan Cruickshank. 2: London Metropolitan Archives. 3, 8–17, 19, 28–32, 34, 36–37, 90: National Monuments Record. 4–7: National Monuments Record Scotland. 18, 22–24, 52, 56, 184–86, 226–28, 230: Mark Fiennes. 20–21: Charles Brooking. 25–27: *Birmingham Post and Mail.* 32: Robin Ollington. 33: Department of the Environment. © Crown copyright, NMR. 35, 54, 147: John Donat. 36: *The Sunday Times.* 38–47: Urban Splash. 49: Ian Beesley. 50–51: Dean Clough Mills. 60, 62–64: Parkview. 61, 67–68: Alex Starkey. 66: Randolph Langenbach. 69: The National Trust. 71–72: *Country Life.* 73–76: Christopher Dalton. 77–89: Keith Parkinson. 96–100: Huw Thomas. 107–08: Kate Peters. 110: *The Times.* 111: Comer Homes. 57–59, 112–13, 149–50, 152–53, 156–58, 160–61,164, 174, 180–81, 195, 212–13, 216, 217–18, 220–22: Marcus Binney. 114: Ev Cooke. 116: Kit Routledge, Richard Pedlar Architects. 117–18: Mitzi de Margary. 120–124: Farnborough Air Sciences Trust. 125–26: Ulster Architectural Heritage Society. 128: James Mortimer. 134–35: Martin Charles. 136: Adam Wilkinson. 137: Lucy Rogers. 139: Jonathan Webb. 143–145: John Gay, with kind thanks to John Murray. 146: Eric de Mare. 148: Savills. 151: Chelmsford Borough Council. 155: DARE. 162–63: Middleton Hall Trust. 166–67: Foster Yeoman Ltd. 168: John Kenworthy-Browne. 169: Heritage Lottery Fund. 173, 201: Dave Wood. 175–76: Kenneth Powell. 177–78: Square Chapel Centre for Arts. 189: www.cressbrookmill.co.uk. 190–92: Ptolemy Dean. 193: Railway Heritage Fund. 197: BH4. 198–99: Linden Homes. 204: Richard Bryant/Arcaid. 205: Richard Rogers Partnership/Eamonn O' Mahony. 224: Peter Higginbotham

CONTENTS

SAVE MISSION STATEMENT

From its launch in 1975 **SAVE** has taken the offensive: publicly fighting applications to demolish historic buildings; demanding that local planners serve repair orders on listed properties left to rot; attacking government departments that fail to carry out basic maintenance on fine architecture in their care; taking legal action against ministers who decline to use the powers Parliament has given them to protect our heritage.

SAVE regularly works with engineers and architects to show how crumbling buildings can be made safe, restored and adapted to lively new uses. *In extremis* **SAVE** has stepped in to acquire key landmarks on death row, repairing them and finding new owners to look after them. Old buildings do not have to be pensioners on the public purse. They can become attractive places to live in and good investments.

Above all, **SAVE** has sought to open eyes to forgotten and unknown places, whether they be dockland warehouses, grand classical barracks or imposing mental hospitals. **SAVE** has championed the great legacy of the railways, the textile mills of the Pennines, ornate Victorian pubs, awesome power stations and the simple dignity of the terrace house. This is a story of triumphs and tragedies; a battle as urgent now as it was 30 years ago.

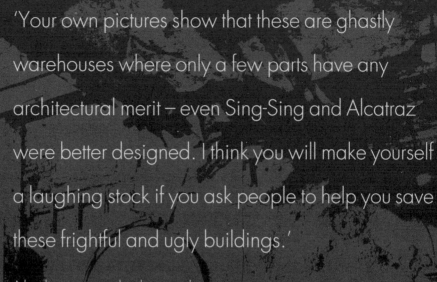

'Your own pictures show that these are ghastly warehouses where only a few parts have any architectural merit – even Sing-Sing and Alcatraz were better designed. I think you will make yourself a laughing stock if you ask people to help you save these frightful and ugly buildings.'

A leading property developer on the
East India Company Warehouses in Cutler
Street, London, 1978

OVER 30 YEARS SAVE HAS:

Published more than 150 reports.

Mounted over a dozen campaigning exhibitions.

Issued more than 400 press releases.

Published an annual catalogue for 16 years of Buildings at Risk.

Started an online subscriber catalogue illustrating over 600 **BUILDINGS AT RISK**.

Initiated successful legal proceedings to save

The Grange, Hampshire;

St Francis Xavier, Liverpool;

Jubilee Hall, Covent Garden, London;

United Reformed Church, Clifton, Bristol.

Taken on and successfully raised finance to restore

Barlaston Hall, Staffordshire;

All Souls, Haley Hill, Halifax;

6 Palace Street, Carnarvon.

SAVE has never received an annual subvention from government.

In lean years it has survived on an annual budget as low as £50,000.

PLEASE SUPPORT SAVE NOW!

Overleaf: The 'Hall of Destruction' in the V&A exhibition *The Destruction of the Country House*, 1974.

SAVE was born out of the immense publicity generated by this now legendary exhibition. The exhibition's 'Hall of Destruction' was a fantasy of tumbling columns, illustrating a selection of over 1000 historic country houses that had been demolished over the preceding century. In 1955 one house was demolished every five days. Such was the concern generated by the exhibition that from 1975 demolition of historic country houses came to a virtual halt.

INTRODUCTION TO SAVE

Marcus Binney, President of **SAVE**

SAVE was conceived primarily to publicise the plight of endangered historic buildings and places. We began in 1975 – European Architectural Heritage Year – with a press release, which announced that in the first eleven weeks of the year local authorities had received applications to demolish 334 listed buildings, as well as 163 located in conservation areas. This was a statistic fuelled by British Rail's application to demolish an entire railway village of nearly 200 houses at Bletchley. It was by no means a piece of scaremongering: permission was indeed given to demolish every house. In Merthyr Tydfil, we pointed out, the Secretary of State for Wales had listed eighty buildings in the town as being of 'special architectural or historic interest'. This was a model village laid out by a local ironmaster in 1807 on an unusual triangular plan. On 25 February, however, the owners (that is, the Council) had applied for permission to demolish all but two of them.

From the start we cast our net wide. Our ninth press release prompted a headline in the *Daily Mirror* 'Spend a Penny for Ye Olde Loo' and, thanks to the publicity, the elegant Edwardian Ladies at Herne Bay, complete with impressive Doric columns, was reprieved.

The spark for the foundation of **SAVE** was the exhibition *The Destruction of the Country House*, which John Harris and I mounted for Roy Strong in the autumn of 1974. The centrepiece of the exhibition was the 'Hall of Destruction', which illustrated a selection of 1,116 houses that had been demolished over the preceding century. In the course of the exhibition that figure grew to 1,600 as a result of further research by Peter Reid.

The V&A Press Office had sent the list of lost houses to every newspaper in the land and during the exhibition we received an avalanche of press cuttings. Hundreds of dailies and weeklies had featured the story of their own lost house. To me this demonstrated that there was an appetite for news stories about endangered heritage and, furthermore, that it was one not being met by any existing organisation.

We held an inaugural meeting to float the idea of what John Harris termed 'a new ginger group' in his handsome Adam office at the RIBA Drawings Collection in Portman Square, December 1974. The response was positive although the Secretary of the Victorian Society said fiercely, 'This mustn't be allowed to go on more than one year

and you aren't to have any members.'

We began by drawing up a budget for an office and paid secretary, which came to £15,000. Initially we had high hopes of raising this in the City but, three months and many begging letters later, we had raised not a penny. As we met in the sitting room of my house in Pimlico in the spring of 1975 it was make or break time so we all decided to put in £10. David Pearce, our vice-chairman, raised a couple of hundred pounds from friends and found us a free office in the basement at 6 Bedford Square. Sarah Seymour became our first volunteer secretary. The manifesto was issued and a long stream of press releases ensued – nearly 100 during our first year. Early releases proclaimed 'Few Days left to save Regency Church', 'Composer's House in Danger', 'Birmingham's Heritage Year Volte Face', 'Watneys Brewery Tower to Go', 'GLC hope to demolish Regency Terrace', 'Permission given to Demolish Handsome Georgian Bank', 'Famous viaduct in Danger', 'Threat to Elizabethan Manor' and 'Hands off Conway Castle'.

Our manifesto, hammered out on a rudimentary portable typewriter, proclaimed, 'The destruction of fine buildings continues despite official conservation policies of recent years…In a period of economic stringency the waste involved in town centre demolitions, for example, is almost criminal. Homes are lost, small businesses destroyed, areas blighted, resources squandered, and the civilising influence of the past dissipated. '

Simon Jenkins, then at the *Evening Standard*, had provided the formula – good punchy copy, statistics and a juicy quote. We gathered lists of endangered buildings from the registers of applications to demolish listed buildings sent to the Society for the Protection of Ancient Buildings. Dan Cruickshank, who worked at the *Architect's Journal*, secured us the opportunity to do the first **SAVE** report in the *Architect's Journal*, with the help of many telling photographs which he had taken or gathered. It was a hard-hitting presentation with a spread of buildings demolished in Heritage Year, set on funeral black and followed by pages of buildings condemned in Heritage Year or simply left to rot.

At the beginning of 1976 Matthew Saunders became **SAVE**'s second secretary and the stream of press releases continued. Later that summer Sophie Andreae succeeded him, devoting her formidable energies to **SAVE** for over a decade. From very early on **SAVE** set out to tackle economic issues. Our first report had highlighted the waste of energy involved in demolishing thousands of terrace houses that could be renovated at less than half the cost of replacing them. In 1976 David Pearce published a **SAVE** report *Conservation and Jobs* in his quarterly *Built Environment*. That December Paul Barker published **SAVE**'s second annual report *The Concrete Jerusalem* in *New Society*: a frontal attack on the devastation caused by comprehensive redevelopment in town and city centres.

Towards the end of summer 1976 **SAVE** issued a press release expressing fears about the sale of Mentmore Towers and the auction of its magnificent collection of Rothschild furniture. Part of the problem was that few people had heard of the house, which had never before been illustrated in *Country Life*. **SAVE** remedied this with its first lightning report, *Save Mentmore for the Nation*, written and published in just a week.

Lord Rosebery had offered to sell his house and its contents to the nation for £2m. At a time of heavy constraint on public expenditure our contention was that the money was already there in departmental budgets, in the form of £1m allocated for museum purchases and another in the Department of the Environment budget for the purchase of historic buildings. This money came from the long-forgotten National Land Fund set up by Hugh

Dalton, the Chancellor of the Exchequer, in 1946. I obtained the thin printed annual reports which, supplemented by Hansard debates, told an extraordinary story that I proceeded to write up in an article *Betrayal of the Fallen* in *Country Life* on 10 March, 1977. Introducing the Fund in the House of Commons on 9 April, 1946 Dalton had said, 'It is surely fitting in this proud moment of our history, when we are celebrating victory and deliverance from overwhelming evils and horrors, that we should make through this fund a thank-offering for victory which in the judgement of many, is better than any work of art in stone or bronze. I should like to think that through this Fund we shall dedicate some of the loveliest parts of this land to the memory of those who died that we might live in freedom.' Eleven years later, when the Fund was under threat from the Treasury, he reiterated his desire for it to be used to ensure that 'the beauty of England, the famous historical houses, the wonderful stretches of still unspoiled countryside, might be preserved. '

As Mentmore's sale approached it became somewhat of a national cause and was debated in Parliament. We lost the battle but won the war. Mentmore's contents were auctioned by Sotheby's but I went on to give evidence for **SAVE** to the Parliamentary Expenditure Committee, maintaining that the Land Fund should be reconstituted under independent trustees. The committee concurred and the result was the establishment of the National Heritage Memorial Fund in April 1980.

In 1977 **SAVE** mounted a combative exhibition at the RIBA's Heinz Gallery *Off the Rails*, which attacked British Rail for its neglect of railway architecture. Peter Parker had just taken over as British Rail's chairman and came to the exhibition, inviting us to what he called 'a sparring match'. Among the results of this debate were the establishment of British Rail's Environment Panel and the appointment of Simon Jenkins to the British Rail Board, which led in turn to the creation of the Railway Heritage Trust to give grants to repairs of listed railway structures.

By this time it had become abundantly clear that, in addition to buildings threatened by an application to demolish, a much larger number were simply standing empty and abandoned or being actively encouraged to fall down by developers. **SAVE**'s response was a trenchant report written by George Allan and Timothy Cantell and published in 1978. It made the case for a much greater use of powers to serve repairs orders on wilfully

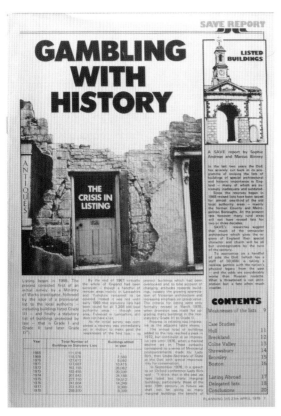

neglected listed buildings; a recurring **SAVE** theme thereafter. With Sophie Andreae as Secretary, **SAVE** also published *Tomorrow's Ruins: Country Houses at Risk*, the first in a long series on buildings of different types falling into decay.

The summer of 1977 saw a second V&A exhibition, *Change & Decay: The Future Of Our Churches*, which Peter Burman, another founding trustee of **SAVE**, and I organised for Roy Strong. To coincide with this **SAVE** published *Churches at Risk*. The exhibition contained copious evidence of the threats to churches, namely to major town churches and remote country churches. Remarkably, within a month of the opening, the Government announced the first grants for historic churches, breaking a longstanding deadlock between Church and State. This owed much to the fact that the Church of England was exempt from listed building controls – as were all other denominations (except where total demolition was involved). Government policy was 'no control, no grants'. Now suddenly the way was open for many millions to flow to both churches and later cathedrals – and for controls to be improved.

Just as *Change & Decay* drew to a close an American preservationist Randolph Langenbach brought in a series of superlative photographs of grand Yorkshire textile mills, which two years later formed the basis of **SAVE** exhibition *Satanic Mills* at the RIBA Heinz Gallery. At this time the Monument Trust, one of our principal financial backers, agreed to support the establishment of a **SAVE** northern office with Ken Powell as northern secretary. Ken found a base in Birchcliffe Centre, a handsome Baptist chapel converted for use by voluntary and community groups, and began a series of cheaply-produced, hard-hitting reports on threats to northern towns and cities. In *City Centre Carve-up* he attacked schemes in Leeds, Liverpool and Newcastle-upon-Tyne for 'commitment to size, to uniformity and to complete renewal, regardless of the economic, visual and human consequences.'

Satanic Mills opened in 1979. We were apprehensive at the reception it might receive. Some local politicians took the line that the mills were unpleasant reminders of a grim past when workers were brutally exploited. To our delight, however, it elicited a tremendously positive reaction, and, thanks to extensive press and radio coverage on both sides of the Pennines, the book of the exhibition sold out within ten days. The books went not to visitors at the exhibition but to local people writing in to make postal orders. Their response was simple: 'These mills are part of our lives. We don't want them torn down.'

The challenge was the sheer number and size of the mills – dozens of four, five and six storey mills in and around towns like Halifax and Huddersfield, and many more tucked into the bottom of valleys snaking up into the Pennines. The greatest obstacle to our progress was mighty Manningham Mills in Bradford, which was to stand empty for over two decades, though the enterprising developers Urban Splash are now beginning renovation. When Ernest Hall's great project for converting the vast Crossley carpet factory, Dean Clough Mills, in the centre of Halifax for small scale enterprises at last became known it represented somewhat of a breakthrough for the northern campaign. At the same time as plans for the factory were emerging, Jonathan Silver conceived a parallel project for Titus Salt's great complex of mills outside Bradford. News of the project was gratefully received by **SAVE**, whose report *Crisis at Saltaire* had been issued in view of the threat of demolition to one of the main mills on the site.

SAVE organised a large travelling version of *Change & Decay*, which toured museums around the country. The exhibition, and accompanying books, highlighted the extraordinary (and until then largely overlooked) quality of dissenting chapels and meeting houses – Baptist, Congregationalist, Methodist, Quaker and Unitarian – and also the range of denominations and fine buildings in Scotland and Wales.

Many of the grandest chapels were in and around the northern mills towns. These formed the subject of Ken Powell's *The Fall of Zion*. **SAVE** was now becoming increasingly involved in sustained battles to prevent decay and demolition; to find new owners and new uses for endangered listed buildings. The battle over The Hazells in Bedfordshire was one of the first. It was in fact this particular campaign which brought us into contact with Kit Martin, then well into his heroic rescue of Dingley Hall in Northamptonshire.

SAVE fielded a strong team at the public inquiry into the Hazells application. The house had been left in a dreadful state when evacuated by the hospital that had taken over there in 1946 but we convinced the inspector that it was practical and viable to restore and convert the house. This verdict was upheld by Michael Heseltine who, ironically, was refusing consent to a fellow Cabinet member, Francis Pym, Secretary of State for Defence. Shortly afterwards Kit Martin acquired the house and restored it as 12 self-contained houses and cottages, much to the satisfaction of all involved.

A major battle to prevent the demolition of Barlaston Hall in Staffordshire followed shortly after the Hazells triumph. Permission had been refused at an earlier inquiry when John Harris and Christopher Buxton had given evidence. This time the owners, Wedgwood, returned with the National Coal Board in support, arguing that not only was the house too far gone to repair but that continuing coal mining would render restoration impractical and prohibitively expensive. SAVE commissioned architect and engineers to show how the house could be stabilised, repaired and converted into seven apartments At the inquiry SAVE's solicitor David Cooper made such a powerful case that Wedgwood's counsel, who had addressed us scathingly as the 'united aesthetes', suddenly flung down the gauntlet and challenged us to buy Barlaston for £1. Perhaps he had hoped to scare us off, but half an hour later Sophie Andreae had agreed the purchase and a delighted inspector proffered the 10p deposit.

Almost simultaneously SAVE commissioned architects and engineers to thwart plans for the demolition of All Souls, Haley Hill: a magnificent church built by the Akroyd family, which towered above the mills of their great rivals, the Crossleys. It was the work of Sir George Gilbert Scott, architect of the Albert Memorial and St Pancras Station Hotel. Scott wrote that he considered it 'his best church'. Ken Powell, who was an ardent student of Gothic Revival, felt passionately about its preservation. We stepped forward, first forming a group of Friends, recruiting Laurence Olivier and Yehudi Menuhin as vice-patrons, and then offering to take a seven-year repairing lease. As our architect we chose the suitably named Donald Buttress, who went on to succeed Peter

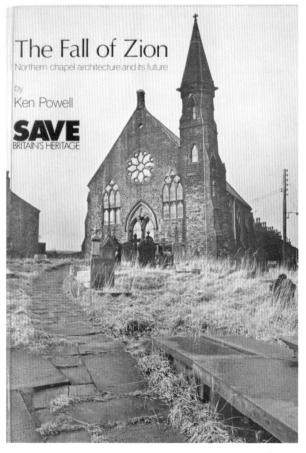

The Fall of Zion
Northern chapel architecture and its future

by
Ken Powell

SAVE
BRITAIN'S HERITAGE

Foster (one of our new trustees) as surveyor to Westminster Abbey.

Donald saw the immediate need to stop rain seeping into the nave roof. He vividly described how loose slates were crashing down and splitting the lead lining of the gutters, allowing moisture into the stonework. He argued that it would take only one more winter for the moisture to reach the roof timbers, at which point there would be an explosion of dry rot. Reroofing with slate would have required a considerable amount of money and time, which we lacked. He determined that it should be done in a blue grey industrial tile (in actual fact a very good colour match) with new eaves oversailing the gutters to throw the rainwater clear. After a furious battle with the Halifax planning officer, who appeared happy to let churches and mills fall down but not to vary his policy on artificial slates, Donald won and the work proceeded. Next came the spire, the second tallest after Louth of any parish church in England. The church authorities had received a report saying it was dangerous and should be taken down lest it topple on a passing bus. With Ove Arup, the engineers, Donald devised a means of strengthening the spire with a single inner skin of brickwork that would not place too much extra weight on the tower below. We applied for a grant from the newly formed National Heritage Memorial Fund, the only possible source of the huge sums needed.

The trustees were seriously split on whether so large a sum should go to a redundant church. It was only Lord Charteris's use of his casting vote as chairman that secured us the funds. Donald never told us that half way through the job, they found an iron ring beam in the spire that had exploded in rust to such an effect that it threatened to topple the tower should it be cut out. Fortunately they devised a means of safely cutting it out in very small sections.

With work on All Souls underway, we embarked on a series of campaigns to save two neo-classical masterpieces on death row: Thomas Harrison's 1803 Lyceum in Liverpool and The Grange in Hampshire. Permission had been given to demolish the Lyceum in 1971. When invited to give a talk in Moscow on public opinion and the preservation of historic buildings at the fifth Assembly of ICOMOS, the International Council on Monuments and Sites, I ended my talk with an appeal to the audience to pay one rouble and sign a telegram to be sent to the British Prime Minister calling for a reprieve for the Lyceum. Years later I had the chance to ask Jim Callaghan about it. Benignly he replied, 'Yes I do remember a telegram. ' That was not the way it seemed at the time; months passed before we received an acknowledgement of a telegram from myself and 'distinguished signatories'. Nonetheless we were able to inject new vigour into the campaign with a report *A Spark Divine: Save the Liverpool Lyceum*. Eventually Peter Shore, the Labour Secretary of State for the Environment, received such an avalanche of letters from Liverpool, many evidently from Labour supporters, that he announced he would revoke the consent to demolish and pay the necessary substantial six figure sum in compensation.

Around much the same time **SAVE** was attacking the Department on The Grange, an august Greek Revival with an architectural roll-call that included Robert Adam, Henry Holland, William Wilkins, George Dance and three members of the Cockerell dynasty. The Grange had been taken into guardianship in 1974 following the huge outcry when demolition began two years earlier, just as a major exhibition on international neo-classicism opened at the Royal Academy. One of **SAVE**'s committee members, the architect John Redmill, had monitored subsequent events and asserted that absolutely no repairs had been carried out. To make the situation even worse, the roof had been stripped of slates, water was pouring in, and the Roman cement was slipping off the columns of the portico in great shards. The explanation was that a particular civil servant had decided The Grange was a waste of public money and should be allowed to fall down. Through Robert Carnwath, who advised and appeared for **SAVE** on many important legal cases, we obtained a copy of the guardianship deed. In this the Secretary of State undertook solemnly to repair the shell and allow access to the public. Our solicitors, Bates, Wells and Braithwaite, wrote to the Minister to say that we would issue a High Court writ of Mandamus, an order requiring a minister to do what statute obliged him to do. Weeks of prevarication ensued until we grew tired and warned that we would go to court the next day. We immediately received notification that the repair work was to commence.

In the space of just a few weeks it seemed as if victory slipped from our grasp. Mrs Thatcher had swept to power and her new Environment Secretary, Michael Heseltine, proceeded to announce a review of whether both these projects justified the sums of public money involved. In response **SAVE** issued another lightning report *Ten Days to Save the Grange*. Michael Heseltine received a large postbag about the buildings, overwhelmingly in favour of preservation, and consequently ruled that both were to be saved.

Two years earlier Peter Shore's junior minister Lady Birk had announced a major cutback on listing. **SAVE** had resolved to publish two well-documented reports: *Gambling with History* and *A Sentence of Mutilation*. The essence of our case was that the initial surveys for listing had been conducted at great speed – listing in Britain began in 1946 while in France it had begun a century earlier – and many buildings had been omitted. A revised survey had been undertaken, to include a selection of Victorian buildings, but this was only one third complete. Once again Michael Heseltine re-examined the issue, decided that a more thorough resurvey was needed, and made available the resources to more than double the total of listed buildings.

SAVE embarked on another battle early in April 1980 to save Billingsgate Fish Market from demolition. The City Corporation were determined to sell the site for redevopment to cover the £7m cost of moving the fish market to Docklands. When Michael Heseltine suddenly spotlisted the building in April 2000 the Corporation reacted with fury. **SAVE** responded by inviting Richard Rogers to prepare a scheme for reuse. This was drawn up by architects Ian Ritchie and Alan Stanton, with major input from the surveyor Hugh Cantlie. With his help we calculated that if an office development was built on the adjoining lorry park the City could more than cover any loss resulting from the preservation of Horace Jones's fine market buildings.

We had to contend with the widespread rumour that, once the cold store in the market was switched off, Billingsgate would simply disappear into the Thames mud as the permafrost beneath it melted, but finally, however, the City Corporation put the fish market up for sale on the basis of a deemed planning permission following the lines we had proposed. A sum of £22m was waived and the Richard Rogers Partnership was called in to carry out the conversion.

Shortly before the battle for Billingsgate was initiated, **SAVE** had begun to express serious concern about another Thames landmark: Battersea Power Station. Initially we had received stonewalling answers from the Central Electricity Generating Board but when we appealed to the Labour Secretary of State, Tony Benn, suddenly all doors were opened. On visiting Battersea in 1979 we found the magnificent turbines of the 1930s Art Deco Turbine Hall already being stripped out. Taken on to lunch at the CEGB headquarters at Bankside Power Station we felt equally impressed and submitted prophetically a proposal to transform it into an art gallery, realised 20 years later with the creation of the Tate Modern. Our report *The Colossus of Battersea* appeared in 1981, with proposals by the architect Martin Richardson and Graham Morrison (now of Allies & Morrison) for converting it for leisure use, with a large sports arena in the huge central boiler house between the four chimneys. Michael Heseltine listed the Power Station. Wandsworth District Council granted **SAVE** permission for leisure use and the battle, which we have always described as the 'Mount Everest of Preservation', commenced.

In addition to fighting individual battles **SAVE** has always been concerned to advance the conservation argument. We did so, importantly, in 1979 with *Preservation Pays: Tourism and the Economic Benefits of Preserving Historic Buildings*. During the 1980s we published three practical reports prepared with architects, aimed at showing how different types of historic buildings could be adapted to imaginative and suitable new uses on a commercially viable basis without the need for grants. The first of these, written with Kit Martin, addressed country houses, the second, *Churches: a Question of Conversion*, included plans by Derek Latham & Associates for sensitively adapting series of churches and chapels. The third, *Bright Futures*, prepared with the architect Francis Machin, showed how derelict mills and warehouses could be transformed and given a new lease of life. A fourth report by Gillian Darley, *A Future for Farm Buildings*, looked at good and bad barn conversions.

In autumn 1982 **SAVE** sprung into action to try and prevent the break-up of another secret treasure house, Calke Abbey in Derbyshire. Using as our campaign poster a glorious photograph of the drawing room taken by Alex Starkey for *Country Life*, we published *This Magical House Must Be Saved Intact, NOW!*. As at Mentmore there were those who both publicly and privately (to ministers) said the house was not worth saving, but the campaign gathered momentum and in his first budget speech in 1984 the Chancellor Nigel Lawson announced that he had no public expenditure announcements, bar one: £4m for Calke Abbey. As this happened, the epic fray over the Mappin & Webb triangle in the City was beginning; a campaign described separately by Jennifer Freeman in the Envoi to this book.

During the 1980s **SAVE** continued to document losses in the spirit of the V&A *Destruction of the Country House* exhibition. *Lost Houses of Scotland* was followed by Tom Lloyd's highly successful *Lost Houses of Wales*. New building types were covered by *Time Gentlemen Please* (on pubs) and *Taking the Plunge: the Architecture of Bathing* – which were both the subject of exhibitions. Meanwhile **SAVE** pursued its documentaries on endangered buildings and places with *Deserted Sepulchres* (on churches, 1983), *Endangered Domains* (on country houses, 1985) and *Garden Temples and Follies: Pavilions in Peril* (1987) and *Scotland's Endangered Houses* (1990).

In 1989 **SAVE**'s secretary Marianne Watson-Smyth compiled *Empty Quarters*, the first of **SAVE**'s now annual catalogues of historic buildings in need of new owners or new uses, followed soon after by *Scotland's Endangered Houses*. In 1993 we launched a major new salvo with *Deserted Bastions*, a report and exhibition at the Heinz Gallery. This was the first attempt at a comprehensive catalogue and survey of architecturally notable military and naval establishments under threat of closure, closed or actually lost. Initially it was a major task for Anthony Peers, our researcher, just to compile the list but as we progressed more help was forthcoming from both the Ministry of Defence and military historians – Jonathan Coad, English Heritage's expert on the architecture of the navy, was a tremendous help from the start. The night after the opening party in April, I set off with the architect Huw Thomas in search of a solution to the crisis of the mighty Peninsula

The
Architects'
Journal

17 & 24
December
1975

25p

What has happened to these historic buildings in European Architectural Heritage Year? See the

SAVE REPORT

Barracks in Winchester. His office was located just opposite, however the great barracks were all but shut off from the town. Worse still, consent had been given to demolish the whole of the lower barracks and replace it with a high density scheme with no certainty as to the fate of the grand classical buildings around the upper parade ground. They echoed Wren's Hampton Court Palace in their columned splendour. Huw drew up an inspired scheme showing how all the buildings could be converted for residential use on a commercial basis, with the parade ground transformed into a formal public garden and a large mirror pool in the centre. This was to be raised above the tarmac to avoid major archaeological excavations. Huw Thomas also proposed replacing the dreary and squat 1960s end block with a reconstruction of the Italianate Victorian officers' mess, which formerly stood at the south end. **SAVE** obtained planning permission for a scheme on these lines, which a few years later was carried through by Try Homes.

At the Ministry of Defence our concerns were taken seriously by the Marquess of

Salisbury (then Lord Cranborne) and policies drawn up to ensure surplus historic buildings were disposed of in a suitable manner. Very different was our experience with the sequel, *Mind over Matter*, the first major study of Mental Hospitals, compiled by **SAVE** Secretary Emma Phillips in 1995. Though economically produced (**SAVE** was very short of funds) this was a catalogue of a group of grand, architectural compositions, some of them featuring on a colossal scale. It was prompted by the fact that by the end of the decade 98 out of 121 mental hospitals would be closed. Many of these asylums were a major exercise in philanthropy. They were usually built on south facing slopes with fine views to ensure a maximum of air and light for the patients. It was often the practice to provide one acre of grounds for every ten patients, with the result that numerous mental hospital stood in fine grounds and among handsome planted trees. Many also had charming wind shelters, like those found on seaside promenades.

SAVE had little cooperation from the Department of Health and the compiling of such an extensive catalogue of grand architecture was an achievement in itself. It quickly transpired that the Department's overriding concern was to sell the sites to housing developers. In obtaining planning permissions, often at considerable expense, the planning consultants involved simply drew up standard suburban housing schemes with no regard for the quality or potential of the standing buildings or, indeed, trees and green spaces. In some cases, where a building was listed, a covenant was imposed preventing its conversion to residential use, so that it would not compete with new housing nearby. This happened at Exvale outside Exeter, where a grand complex of Georgian buildings on a hemicycle plan, with finger wings projecting outwards, was allowed to fall into a catastrophic state. English Heritage stepped in to oversee the repairs, which cost a substantial six-figure sum. Since then, the whole complex has been renovated by Davington Homes.

In 1994 **SAVE** issued an outraged response to the Templeman report, which had listed 27 City of London churches as potential candidates for closure, mothballing or secular use. The list included several of Sir Christopher Wren's finest churches, rebuilt after the Great Fire of London in 1666. **SAVE**'s report *The City Churches Have a Future* led directly to the establishment of the Friends of the City Churches, who now regularly provide volunteers to enable churches to be open to the public. As such, not one church has been closed.

The **SAVE** reports on defence and hospital buildings helped lead to a long stream of successful conversions. They include Kit Martin's rescue of the Royal Naval Hospital in Great Yarmouth, the transformation of Shoeburyness Barracks into a model town of hundreds of houses in restored buildings, the retention and conversion of a substantial part of the Guards' barracks at Caterham, none of which were listed. Among the major hospitals that have been successfully converted to residential use are the Royal Earlswood Hospital near Redhill, the Royal Holloway Sanitorium near Virginia Water, and the large mental hospitals at Colney Hatch, Haywards Heath and Maidstone. Near Plymouth, Moorhaven Hospital was taken over by two young surveyors who have transformed the complex into a flourishing village on the edge of Dartmoor.

Blink and You'll Miss It was written by **SAVE** Secretary Richard Pollard in 2001: a highly critical report on conservation, or the lack of it, in Northern Ireland, published with a wealth of documentation supplied by the doughty Ulster Architectural Heritage Society. This highlighted a series of scandals including the delisting of listed buildings simply because of unsuitable alterations to windows, the complete failure to serve repairs notices on listed buildings left to decay, the failure to prosecute developers who demolished listed buildings without consent, sometimes flagrantly, and the lack of any form of spotlisting in Ulster for imminently endangered historic buildings.

Since 1978, when *Left to Rot* was published, **SAVE** has been systematically pressing local planning authorities to employ their powers to serve repairs notices. In the early years there was a widespread reluctance to use these powers for fear that the local council would then have to purchase the building if there were no beneficial use for it. In fact this rarely happened. The more usual scenario is that, on receipt of a repairs' notice, the owner offers the house for sale on the open market. In this campaign **SAVE** has been greatly helped by the so-called 'Heseltine clause'. Inserted into planning circulars from the early 1980s, it has achieved that consent will not normally be granted to demolish a listed building unless it has been offered for sale on the open market at a price reflecting its condition. In May 2005 **SAVE**'s *Buildings at Risk* officer Ela Palmer organised a

conference attended by 90 local authority lawyers and conservation officers on the subject of enforcement procedures for endangered historic buildings.

SAVE became embroiled in a new battle in early 2003 over a great Victorian country house, Tyntesfield, south of Bristol. While Georgian country houses, complete with their contents and collections, survive in impressive numbers, the opposite is the case for grand Victorian mansions, many of which have been transformed into institutions. Mark Girouard, doyen of country house historians, was asked by the National Trust to provide a list of great Victorian country houses, as potential candidates for the National Trust, in terms of their quality and completeness. First came Cragside, acquired by the Trust in 1977, and second was Tyntesfield. Unfortunately the late Lord Wraxall had left his estate divided between 19 heirs, none of whom could buy out the others.

SAVE's report *The Tyntesfield Emergency* had to be produced amidst severe difficulties. Many of those who had visited the house recently and were best qualified to write about it had signed undertakings not to make public comment about it. Only a limited number of photographs was available. There was an almost impossible deadline of less than two months in which to clinch an agreement to acquire the tout ensemble. Failing that, a Christie's sale would proceed. Under a dynamic new director-general, Fiona Reynolds, The National Trust, initially hesitant to take the house without a partner such as English Heritage, stiffened its resolve, entered negotiations with determination and for the first time agreed to take a great house without an endowment allowing time for further negotiations over educational and community programmes that might attract financial support.

SAVE has consistently set out to champion the cause of those buildings and places whose significance is not rightly appreciated. A current example is the Royal Aircraft Establishment at Farnborough, widely known as the cradle of British aviation. Farnborough was a top secret establishment, akin to Bletchley Park where the code breakers worked, a place where information was provided on a need-to-know basis. **SAVE**'s report *Enough Has Been Bulldozed* illustrated the magnificent wind tunnels and argued that the historic core of the site should be preserved as an urban village at the heart of the major new office development being planned by the new owners Slough Estates. The **SAVE** scheme has now been adopted by Slough Estates, who are spending £20m on renovation.

SAVE's report *Silence in Court* by Richard Pollard is an extensive catalogue of law courts of all types, including many of the finest Assizes courthouses and magistrates courts in Britain, and illustrates some of the fine interiors for the first time. A number of the surviving courts are as handsomely and intricately laid out as a box-pewed Georgian church, with a tiered public gallery to allow a good view of the proceedings. **SAVE** was concerned that many traditional courts were being closed or stripped out and replaced by new courts, which were often remarkably similar in layout to older ones. Our contention is that a good architect can often adapt an older court sympathetically, meeting new requirements for secluded space for witnesses and lawyers.

Currently **SAVE** is fighting a sustained battle over the market buildings at the west end of Smithfield. These include the old General Market and, unexpectedly, a Fish Market, announced by a delightful statue of a boy on a dolphin. They are linked by a delightful wooden fretted canopy of the railway type. This is an unusual and charming townscape feature but the developers Thornfield, who are seeking to build offices on the site, have applied for consent to demolish this. Astonishingly Thornfield and the City instead want to replace the western market building with a slab block, hardly distinguishable from those built along Farringdon Road in the 60s and 70s, making it one of London's grimmest thoroughfares. They are also pursuing the delisting of the recently listed cold store. Significantly, one of the last acts of the Greater London Council before it was abolished was to extend the Smithfield conservation area to include these buildings. Tessa Jowell, the Secretary of State for Culture, has stated that a public inquiry should be held into any application to demolish these buildings. The whole Smithfield quarter, like neighbouring Clerkenwell, is a superb example of natural regeneration; of older buildings being given a new lease of life by enlightened landlords and lively small businesses. If market stalls in the handsome arcades within the General Market and the Fish Market were available for rent they would be snapped up as quickly as those in Borough Market where there is now a two-year waiting list.

An experienced MP once said, 'If you want to save old buildings you must do it by stealth. As soon as it becomes a public issue there will be cries of what a waste of taxpayers' or ratepayers' money.' **SAVE**'s work is premised on the belief that large numbers of people do care passionately about the historic buildings surrounding them. As we said in our 1975 manifesto, 'There is ample evidence that more and more people *care*. **SAVE** aims to make sure that more and more people *know* in time to help.' **SAVE** understands that old buildings do not need to be pensioners . The vast majority can become good investments and attractive places in which to live and work, as well as serving a whole range of recreational purposes, as with, exotically, the water-pumping station in north London transformed into an indoor climbing centre.

SAVE's online catalogue of *Buildings at Risk* attracts thousands of visitors every year who are looking for places to restore, whether to live in, rent or sell. The BBC's *Restoration* series recognised the vast number of people who are interested not just in visiting but in helping to find ways of breathing life into local landmarks.

SAVE remains dedicated to seeing through the first crucial stages of the restoration process, giving initial publicity and speaking out for the quality and interest of the building, and the practicality of preserving it. On other occasions, however, we have also worked with engineers and architects to show that collapse can be avoided, drawing up plans for repair and reuse. Very often our role extends to supporting local people who are struggling to get their case heard or to be taken seriously. Whether it is a local landmark like a school, a pub or a swimming pool, a fine historic country house or church, **SAVE** is eager to hear about it.

We have never shied away from fighting developments that are overscaled, badly designed or unsympathetic to their surroundings. Nevertheless, we are constantly on the lookout for architects and developers who are sensitive to historic buildings and structures. We have, for example, supported Sapcotes, who have made a speciality of school buildings, especially Victorian Board schools, converting them into apartments; and P. J. Livesey, a company that has taken on major houses such as Wyfold Court and Ingress Abbey near Dartford.

Many of the 'problem' country houses now coming to **SAVE** have spent 15 to 30 years in institutional use, during which time they have often become enveloped by unsuitable extensions – as caricatured so well by Osbert Lancaster for the *Destruction of the Country House*. Few developers, however, are willing to let the footprint of such extensions lapse. The challenge is in finding a way to move replacement development out of the view of the house without simply allowing for another scene to be spoiled. **SAVE** is therefore particularly pleased to have enlisted DARE as sponsor for this book and the exhibition that will accompany this exhibition.

DARE has made a speciality of sorting out problem country houses, of obtaining planning permissions to removed unsightly developments, of seeking to site and design new buildings discreetly and sympathetically. Recently they have acquired Georgian Axwell Park, south of Newcastle, designed by the architect James Paine. After World War II Axwell Park served as a borstal but the house has stood empty since the late 1970s and has been badly vandalised. In the basement is a Quatermass-style dry rot fruiting body, 20 feet in diameter. Warders' houses have been built along the drive and a crude school block was added, breaking through the walled garden. DARE plans to convert the main house into 23 apartments, demolish the crude additions, with a view to replacing their footprint with a new Palladian block on the site of the old stables and a series of contemporary houses in the walled garden, where the lost walls will be rebuilt.

For **SAVE**, after 30 years of campaigning, the greatest news to arrive is that there have never been more enterprising individuals and organisations interested in tackling historic buildings, both large and small. Yet the threats will never go away.

SAVE's current secretary, Adam Wilkinson, has played a major role in fighting the Government's proposals to demolish up to 100,000 traditional terrace houses in the north of England. This is one of most brutal pieces of social engineering since the forced highland clearances of the nineteenth century. Residents are being forced out of their homes against their will, their houses condemned on the basis of a superficial external survey that has often lasted no more than a few minutes. So-called consultations take place during working hours when most residents cannot attend. Many residents who have invested heavily in their homes find them blighted by the newly vacated properties around them. Great distress is caused to older people who have lived in these homes all their lives only to now be offered a new house, which is too expensive, and a mortgage they cannot afford.

The absurdity of Pathfinder (the name itself is a dubious crib from a Sunday school programme) is nowhere more evident than in the claim that there is no market for many of these northern houses. It is also, spuriously, argued that they represent a negative value; that they will cost more to modernise than they will be worth when the job is completed. Since these dubious calculations were first made the value of many of these houses has doubled or trebled. The reason why the Government is so reluctant to rein in Pathfinder, despite increasing comment to the contrary, appears simple: vested interests. Primarily there are the consultants with their fat fees, amounting to a staggering £163m according to Regeneration minister Jeff Rooker in evidence to Parliament in February 2005. Secondly the housing associations, which are in many cases the registered social landlords, are buying up streets of traditional housing in order to create landbanks not

for housing the needy but to sell on to commercial developers. In the process of running down whole areas they are not only driving down prices but depriving householders of a fair price when they are forced to sell or leave their homes.

The saving of historic buildings is often comparable to a relay race, with successive people taking up the baton and running with it. This book illustrates just a fraction of the hundreds and hundreds of town and country houses, cottages and farmhouses, churches and chapels, buildings of almost every type, which have been highlighted in **SAVE** reports or included in our online register of buildings at risk. An encouraging number of these, certainly the majority, have found a new lease of life. When the battle is won, those who fought in the early stages are often forgotten. We perceive our role as having always been in conservation's front line. The cases that follow represent just a selection of the delightful, charming, unusual historic buildings that we have championed. We hope they will inspire you to join **SAVE** and join the fight.

CAMPAIGNS

SOME HISTORIC BUILDINGS CAN BE SAVED BY A SINGLE WELL-TIMED PRESS

RELEASE OR ARTICLE. OTHERS REQUIRE SUSTAINED CAMPAIGNS TO SECURE A

REPRIEVE. **SAVE** HAS MADE THE CASE FOR PUBLIC FUNDS TO ENABLE THE

NATIONAL TRUST TO ACQUIRE GREAT HOUSES IN DANGER OF BREAK-UP, AND

IN THE LAST RESORT HAS STEPPED IN ITSELF TO ACQUIRE AND RESCUE FINE

BUILDINGS ON DEATH ROW.

BIRTH OF SAVE

In the first six months of 1975 permission was given to demolish no less than 182 listed buildings in England and Wales; and this was European Architectural Heritage Year. **SAVE** press releases and reports documented their destruction.

1 Westminster Palace Hotel under destruction, 1975. The finest hotel in London when it opened in 1860, it was not listed. First **SAVE** report in the *Architects' Journal*, December 1975.

2 Daniel Asher Alexander's magnificent London Docks under demolition, c. 1975.

3 The splendid 1877 Brown & Pank Warehouse which stood guard at the entrance to Northampton, demolished in 1975, the year of this photograph.

THE SAVE REPORT
Heritage year toll

In the first six months of 1975 permission was given to demolish no less than 182 buildings in England and Wales listed by the DOE as being of special architectural or historic interest. Hundreds more were partially demolished or drastically altered and their settings ruined. This means that listed buildings are now disappearing at a rate of one per day—a dramatic acceleration over the 276 buildings lost in 1974 and the 226 in 1972. Even given the fact that more buildings are being placed on the 'lists' each year, the loss suggests a disturbing inability on the part of the authorities to protect the very buildings they have singled out as worthy of preservation. At this rate, 10 000 buildings officially classed as 'historic' will disappear over the next 25 years.

Faced with this potential loss it is hardly surprising that the UK Heritage Year poster proclaims the aim of calling the attention of the European 'peoples to the steady erosion of their common architectural heritage': as far as Britain is concerned the results have been a sham. Heritage Year has provided yet another occasion—of which there are already far too many—for Britain's architects, town planners and local authorities to pat each other on the back and give themselves awards. While the country's heritage has been vanishing at an ever faster rate, our stone centres have been sprouting costumblised precincts, flower boxes and congratulatory receptions. Hardly a warning note has been sounded about the 'erosion' of anything, except perhaps the ratepayer's purse.

Heritage Year has possibly been unfortunate in coinciding with a year of economic recession unprecedented since the second world war. As a result many local councils simply abandoned their Heritage Year projects. The DOE, which had so ardently supported the idea of Heritage Year, found itself effectively ordering local authorities to ignore it, under the guise of cutting out all 'unnecessary' expenditure. The list of projects put forward to celebrate Heritage Year—projects which should in any civilised community have been normal civic activities—makes pathetic reading. This emphasis on spending public money on

superficialities was fundamentally mistaken: the campaign should have pressed instead for the use of legal sanctions that now lie dormant, and for fiscal reforms that would encourage owners to maintain and use their buildings in the public interest.

Most depressing of all—and this message shines through our report—Heritage Year has not rarely been accompanied by any increased sense of responsibility on the part of the public authorities which are themselves increasingly the custodians of historic buildings. The local authority and the public corporation have assumed the grim mantle of vandalism which once lay on the shoulders of the private property developer. For, given an alert public opinion and a determined local authority, there is precious little which a private property developer can get away with. Yet Britain is also cursed with some of Europe's most philistine public officials. Some of the cases quoted below of vandalism and neglect of buildings within the public sector ought by rights to entail the impeachment of some publicly elected or appointed officials. The fact that they can and do claim to be acting in the public's name and with the public's best interests at heart makes the menace they pose all the more threatening. We hope that by detailing both specific cases and the general principles arising out of them we have shed some light on what must now be considered the biggest area of threat to Britain's architectural heritage. We hope that we have done something to redress the balance of Heritage Year in its patent failure to live up to its stated promise.

The Westminster Palace Hotel in Victoria Street, Westminster, was the finest and largest hotel in London when it was opened in 1860. After the first world war it was converted into offices and renamed Abbey House. Despite it being a pioneer building, and despite its historic interest and fine marble and plaster staircase, the building was not listed and was demolished earlier this year.

1

2

3

'Heritage Year has provided yet another occasion – of which there
are already far too many – for Britain's architects, town planners and
local authorities to pat each other on the back and give themselves
awards. While the country's heritage has been vanishing at an ever
faster rate, our town centres have been sprouting cosmeticised
precincts, flower boxes and congratulatory receptions.'

First **SAVE** report in *the Architects' Journal,* 1975

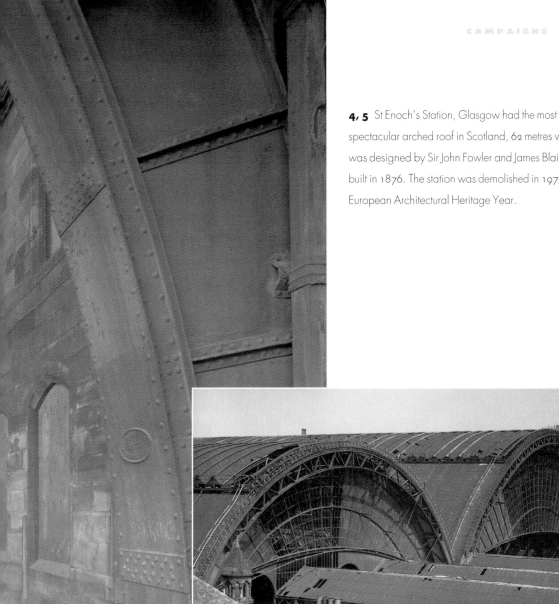

4, 5 St Enoch's Station, Glasgow had the most spectacular arched roof in Scotland, 62 metres wide. It was designed by Sir John Fowler and James Blair and built in 1876. The station was demolished in 1975, European Architectural Heritage Year.

5

THE EMPTY COUNTRY HOUSES

Early **SAVE** reports put the spotlight on beautiful
houses which had been left empty or allowed to
descend into pitiful decay, often by absentee
owners who hoped to develop the sites. As a
result of sustained publicity and pressure many of
these houses have successfully found new owners
and new uses. No less important, local authorities
were persuaded to use powers given to them by
Parliament to serve repairs orders.

6

6, 7 Mavisbank in Victorian times and shortly after it
was gutted by fire in 1973. **SAVE** financed a successful
legal challenge when the house was threatened with
immediate demolition under a Dangerous Structures
Notice. Built 1723 – 27 to the designs of William
Adam.

8 Hellaby Hall, near Rotherham, Yorkshire. A 'swagger Baroque' house of the 1690s, left empty and decaying.

9 Belford Hall, Northumberland, designed by James Paine and completed in 1756. Owned by a gravel extraction company, this handsome Palladian villa fell into a desperate state before rescue by the Monument Trust in the 1980s.

10 Stayley Hall, Manchester, abandoned yet noble nonetheless. A grand, symmetrically gabled house of the 1570s, probably built for Sir William Booth.

8

'Since **SAVE** published *Tomorrow's Ruins: Country Houses at Risk* in 1978 more than two-thirds of the 56 houses included have found new owners or new uses.'

Silent Mansions: More Country Houses at Risk, 1981

9

10

11 Sinai Park, Staffordshire, a magnificent timber-framed house nearing collapse. Built in the early 16th century, possibly as a summer residence for the abbots of Burton Abbey.

CHURCHES UNDER FIRE

As city centres were bulldozed for
redevelopment, fine Victorian churches
were left isolated and vandalised.
Dozens of remote country churches were
also declared redundant. Many were
demolished but the V&A's campaigning
exhibition *Change & Decay*, in 1977,
triggered the first grants for historic
churches. **SAVE**'s travelling version of the
exhibition toured Britain for three years,
followed in 1979 by *The Fall of Zion*, a
powerful plea for northern chapels and
meeting houses.

12 Eckington Methodist Chapel, Derbyshire, shortly
before demolition in 1977.

13, 14 Brunswick Methodist Church, Leeds, built
1824 – 25 to the designs of Joseph Botham. The
magnificent galleried interior with its grand organ was
still splendidly maintained in the early 1960s, but the
church was closed soon after and badly vandalised.
Though **SAVE** campaigned for its retention, permission
to demolish was given after a public inquiry in 1980.

12

13

14

15

16

15, 16, 17 St Clement's, Sheepscar, Leeds, by
George Corson, 1868. The best high Victorian church
in Leeds. Though it had a lively congregation, it was
abruptly closed in 1975. It was then vandalised and set
on fire. The fine organ case by J.F. Bentley was
tragically destroyed. Listed in 1974, it was demolished
two years later.

17

18

18 St Paul's, Cross Stone, West Yorkshire, 1830s.
A standard church commissioners' design in a simple
lancet style, by Matthew Oakes and Thomas
Pickersgill. When it was declared redundant in 1980,
SAVE obtained permission for residential use and it is
now a house.

19 Unitarian Church, St Vincent Street, Glasgow.
Designed in the form of a Roman temple by J. Burnet,
1850, it was demolished in 1983 for an office
development.

19

FIGHT FOR LONDON TOWN HOUSES

In 1980 the Chinese Embassy in Portland Place, designed by Robert Adam, was demolished under the pretext of diplomatic immunity. Meanwhile, hundreds of Georgian houses in Islington and neighbouring boroughs, many owned by the council, were left empty and allowed to decay. **SAVE** successfully campaigned with local people to prevent the demolition of 29 Regency houses in Shepherdess Walk, Hackney, shown overleaf handsomely restored by a housing association.

20, 21 The Chinese Embassy at 50 Portland Place under demolition in 1980. The exterior has since been rebuilt in replica. The house was built to the designs of the Adam brothers c. 1785.

20

21

22, 23, 24 Regency terrace houses in Shepherdess Walk, Hackney, London. Shown restored, and (below opposite) derelict.

'These houses are absolutely finished and we really need the open space.'

A local councillor on Shepherdess Walk, 1975

23

24

BATTLE JOINED ON RAILWAY ARCHITECTURE

25

The loss of the Euston Arch in 1962 marked the beginning of an onslaught. Modernisation, line closures and simple neglect took a devastating toll on railway architecture, leading to the demolition of grand city stations like Bradford and St Enoch's in Glasgow, as well as handsome stations in market towns and major viaducts.

26

SAVE's combative exhibition *Off the Rails* in 1977, coinciding with Sir Peter Parker's appointment as chairman of British Rail, brought a transformation in attitudes. It was followed in 1984 by the establishment of the Railway Heritage Trust, which has given more than £20m in grants to listed structures.

25, 26, 27 The Great Western Hotel at Birmingham Snow Hill Station, built in 1852, converted to the regional railway office in 1905, and demolished in 1970. The abandoned Victorian platform canopies were also demolished.

'Britain invented the railway, pioneered its application to passenger travel and built the most extensive network of lines and stations anywhere in the world. We also did so earlier than anyone else. As a result, Britain's railways constitute an architectural and archaeological achievement without parallel.'

Simon Jenkins, in the introduction to *Off the Rails*

28 Birkenhead Woodside Station by R. E. Johnston, 1878. The ticket hall before demolition in 1969.

29 Derby Station, the home of the Midland Railway. The grand classical front of the 1890s was demolished in 1985, despite strong objections from **SAVE**.

29

MENTMORE TOWERS: A BATTLE LOST, A WAR WON

In 1977 **SAVE** launched a vigorous campaign to stop the auction of Mentmore's rich collections, demanding that the government should finance purchase from the £13m in the National Land Fund set up in 1946. Despite mounting public outcry, ministers refused to act. In the end, they spent as much on individual treasures for museums as it would originally have cost to buy house and contents together. The Parliamentary Environment Committee intervened and adopted **SAVE**'s proposal that the Land Fund should be an independent body, leading to the formation of the National Heritage Memorial Fund in 1980.

30

30 The Great Hall at Mentmore. A record photograph taken shortly before the sale.

31 Mentmore Towers, Buckinghamshire, built 1852 – 54 to the designs of Sir Joseph Paxton and his son-in-law G.H. Stokes for Baron Meyer Amschel de Rothschild. The design was based on the Elizabethan mansion Wollaton Hall but incorporated hot water and artificial ventilation throughout.

31

32

32 Cartoon of Mentmore sale by Robin Ollington.

'It is surely fitting, in this proud moment of our history, when we are celebrating victory and deliverance from overwhelming evils and horrors, that we should make through this fund a thank-offering for victory, and a war memorial which…is better than any work of art in stone or bronze.'

Hugh Dalton, Chancellor of the Exchequer, 1946

'In 1945 and 1946 we were selling vast quantities of war stores…I wished…to set aside some part of that so that the beauty of England, the famous historical houses, the wonderful stretches of still open country, might be preserved in the future.'

Hugh Dalton, 1957

THE GRANGE RESCUED FROM IMMINENT COLLAPSE

This great Neo-classical house at Northington, Hampshire was taken into guardianship by the government as a result of fierce public outcry when demolition began in 1972. For seven years The Grange was allowed to crumble until **SAVE** took legal action to force ministers to repair it and open it to the public, as they had solemnly undertaken to do. The Grange is now home to a highly successful summer opera festival.

33, 34 The Grange restored to splendour by the Department of the Environment following a legal action by **SAVE**.

33

34

'In terms of international Neo-classicism The Grange compares to the Madeleine in Paris or the Admiralty in Leningrad. It is to the history of country house design what David's *Oath of the Horatii* is to the history of painting or Canova's *Maria Christina Monument* in Vienna is to funerary sculpture.'

SAVE report *Ten Days to Save The Grange*

35, 36, 37 The Grange is a Greek Revival masterpiece, built to the designs of William Wilkins for the banker Henry Drummond 1804 – 09. It was later extended by Sir Robert Smirke and C.R. Cockerell. Bottom left, the house before demolition began. Top left, after demolitions was halted in 1974 and, right, the interior as it was left at the time.

35

36

'Viewed from the ground opposite… nothing can be finer, more classical or like the finest Poussin.'

The architect C. R. Cockerell on visiting The Grange, 1823

SAVING SATANIC MILLS

Blackened and brooding, the hundreds of grand Victorian and Edwardian textile mills in the Pennines looked like a species in danger of extinction. In 1979 **SAVE**'s exhibition *Satanic Mills* showed that many local people felt enormous pride in these great buildings. Thanks to the efforts of entrepreneurs like Ernest Hall at Dean Clough in Halifax, Jonathan Silver at Saltaire and now Urban Splash at Manningham Mills, many of them have been given a dynamic new lease of life, as space for small enterprises, art galleries and residential apartments.

38

38 The fireworks display marking the launch of Urban Splash's conversion of Manningham Mills.

39 To celebrate the completion of Manningham Mills, the directors held a dinner at the top of the chimney, which was designed in emulation of a grand Italian campanile.

41

42   43

40, 41, 42, 43 Manningham Mills, Bradford,
exterior and interior before restoration. Designed by
Bradford architects Andrews & Pepper and built in
the 1870s, the mills dominate the Bradford skyline.
After standing empty for years they are now being
restored as apartments by Urban Splash.

44

45

44, 45, 46, 47 Show apartment demonstrating how Manningham Mills are being converted to residential use, leaving the brick-arched fireproof vaults exposed to view.

48

48 Nahum's Mill, Salterhebble, near Halifax, before demolition.

49 Machinery being dismantled at Salt's Mill, Saltaire, West Yorkshire.

50 The Henry Moore Gallery at Dean Clough.

51 Dean Clough Mills, Halifax. The huge complex of carpet mills built by the Crossley family date from 1841. They were empty and derelict when they were finally acquired by the musician and entrepreneur Sir Ernest Hall and his son Jeremy. These days 100 companies operate from there, employing over 3,500 people.

49

52 Hunslet Mill in Leeds, overlooking River Aire. Prime candidate for restoration as apartments.

53 Clark Bridge Mill, Halifax, as demolition began in the 1980s.

52

53

'Two hundred chimneys, each one the heaven-storming symbol of the pride and prestige of the company that owned it, rose over the mass of housing and factories. The sight of these chimneys, on the rare clear days when they could be seen, must have been staggering, and it remains so even today, after the felling of over half of them.'

Randolph Langenbach on Oldham, *Satanic Mills*

ONE HOUSE, MANY HOMES

The Hazells, the handsome Georgian seat of the Pym family, was leased as a hospital in 1947 and left in a dreadful state when suddenly vacated 21 years later. The Pym family had built a new house on the other side of the beautiful Repton park and applied for consent to demolish. At a public inquiry in 1979 **SAVE** argued forcefully that the house could be restored, without grants, for several families to live in. When consent to demolish was refused the house was sold to Kit Martin who converted the buildings into 12 houses, cottages and flats.

54

54, 55 The Hazells in 1981 before repairs began.

56 The entrance front as restored by Kit Martin.

55

56

DESTRUCTION OF AN ART DECO MASTERPIECE

Threatened with redevelopment, the 1930s Firestone Factory was about to be listed when bulldozers were brought in over a Bank Holiday weekend in August 1980 to gouge out the handsome centrepiece of the long stylish façade. This was the work of the architect Thomas Wallis. Michael Heseltine, Secretary of State for the Environment was so angry with Trafalgar House, the owners of the factory, that he promptly listed the Guildhall School of Music, which the company was then seeking to redevelop in addition to a series of key 1930s landmarks that included the Hoover Factory, also by Thomas Wallis.

57, 59 The Firestone Factory in 1980, shortly before demolition by Trafalgar House, owners of the *Daily Express* whose Fleet Street office was another Art Deco masterpiece.

58 The Factory after the centrepiece of the long frontage had been gouged out. Workers had left their offices on the Friday evening with no knowledge of imminent demolition.

59

58

57

'West of Syon Lane the ultra modern factories standing back amidst green lawns…look so ornate that they might easily be mistaken for the mansions of merchant princes and potentates of some great city in the East.'

Harold Clunn, *London Marches On*, 1946

In 1981 **SAVE** led the campaign to prevent the demolition of Battersea Power Station, obtaining first its Grade II listing and then planning permission for leisure use. **SAVE**'s proposals were drawn up by architects Martin Richardson and Graham Morrison. Parkview, the present owners, have commissioned new designs for a shopping and leisure complex in the power station and have announced a start by 2006. Meanwhile **SAVE**'s parallel proposal (made in 1981) for converting Sir Giles Gilbert Scott's Bankside Power Station into an art gallery has been triumphantly realised with the opening of Tate Modern.

60 Cross section of the power station, showing current proposals by Parkview International for reuse. The former boiler house between the chimneys will become a major space for events, while the turbine hall on either side will be transformed into shopping malls.

61 The power station by night from across the River Thames.

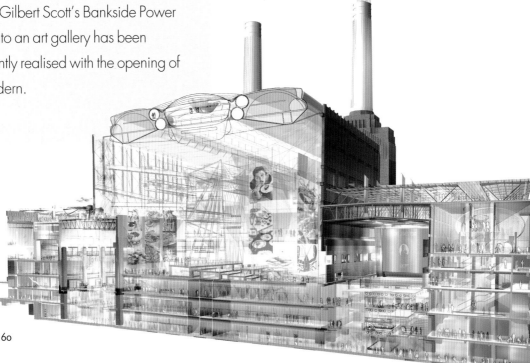

60

62

62, 63, 64 Proposals for converting the turbine halls into shopping centres with a restaurant in the 1930s Art Deco Control Room.

'When the editor of *The Times Diary* asked, half in jest, for suggestions as to what should be done, he was overwhelmed with the response. "One thing is certain," he wrote, "Londoners love Battersea Power Station."'

SAVE report *The Colossus of Battersea*, 1981

63

64

65

65 Bankside Power Station, now transformed into Tate
Modern.

66 Interior of the 1930s turbine hall at Battersea,
shortly after the power station had been decom-
missioned and the massive turbines stripped out.

CALKE ABBEY CAMPAIGN

Calke Abbey in Derbyshire was a secret house where time had stood still for a century and nothing had been thrown away. What one critic described as 'skiploads of junk' transpired to include Bronze Age swords, silver by Paul de Lamerie, an autograph musical score by Haydn and an eighteenth-century state bed with pristine silk hangings still in their wrapping. Following a vigorous **SAVE** campaign, the chancellor Nigel Lawson used his budget speech in 1984 to announce a grant of £5m to enable the National Trust to take over the house.

'The secrecy of Calke is astonishing, considering that it stands within twenty miles of Nottingham, Derby, Leicester and Burton-on-Trent.'

John Harris, **SAVE** report *This Magical House Must be Saved Intact NOW!*

69

67, 68 Calke Abbey, the home of the Harpur-Crewe family, secluded in its deer park. The entrance front was built in 1701 – 03 for Sir John Harpur by an unknown architect. The portico by William Wilkins was added 1806 – 08.

69 The early 18th-century state bed at Calke Abbey. Though its existence was known, this was only discovered to be complete when chosen as an exhibit for the *Treasure Houses of Britain* exhibition in Washington DC in 1985. The fabrics are in pristine condition, as they were kept in store for nearly three centuries. The hangings are of embroidered Chinese silk. It is said that the bed was a present to George II's daughter Anne on her marriage to the Prince of Orange in 1734, and that she then gave it to a bridesmaid who married Sir Henry Harpur of Calke Abbey.

70 SAVE's campaign poster for Calke Abbey. This shows the drawing room, with the 19th-century textiles and wallpaper retaining their original brilliance. In the SAVE report, this was described by Gervase Jackson-Stops as 'one of the few absolutely authentic rooms of this date to remain intact'.

70

"The most pristine Victorian room in Britain"

Calke Abbey

This magical house must be saved intact NOW!

BARLASTON HALL

This imposing Palladian villa in
Staffordshire had been boarded up for
ten years and badly damaged by coal
mining subsidence when **SAVE** bought it
for £1 at a public inquiry in 1981. **SAVE**
had to take legal proceedings to force the
Department of the Environment and the
National Coal Board to pay monies
promised for repairs.

With the help of engineer Brian Morton,
the house was placed on a raft to protect
it from further subsidence. When
structural repairs were complete and all
the distinctive octagonal windows
repaired, **SAVE** put the house on the
market. It was bought by James and
Carol Hall, who have restored the
remarkable Rococo interiors and taken
responsibility for the parish church which
SAVE had acquired to forestall demolition
by the Coal Board.

71

74 The house shortly after **SAVE** bought it for £1 in 1981. Built 1756 – 58, almost certainly to the designs of Sir Robert Taylor. Though the house was in an extreme state of dereliction, the distinctive octagonal and diamond sash windows, almost Rococo in character, had survived untouched since the house was built.

75 The derelict library. Though filled with debris from collapsed ceilings, the mahogany bookcase fronts, with their distinctive octagonal glazing, survived largely intact.

75

76 The dining room soon after **SAVE** acquired the house.

76

ALL SOULS, HALEY HILL, HALIFAX

All Souls, Haley Hill, Halifax, was built 1856 – 59 to the designs of Sir George Gilbert Scott. To forestall demolition of this great Victorian church **SAVE** set up a trust and took a seven-year lease. It strengthened the endangered spire with the help of a major grant from the National Heritage Memorial Fund.

77, 79 Scott's magnificent spire, the second highest of any parish church in England. The roof was leaking badly, threatening a major outbreak of dry rot.

78 The new nave roof carefully matches the colour of the old slates and is designed to throw rainwater over the parapets.

77

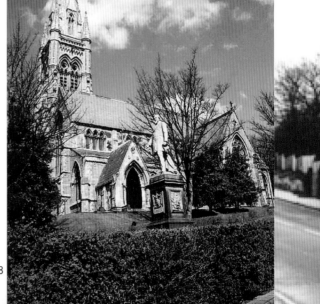

78

80

80, **81** No maintenance has been carried out since
the church closed in 1977 and the stonework was in
a parlous state.

NORTHERN PUBS

These atmospheric photographs of pubs in Liverpool, Leeds and Nottingham were commissioned for **SAVE**'s 1983 exhibition *Time Gentlemen Please!* They highlight the remarkable but highly vulnerable interiors with their original fixtures and furnishings.

82 The Boy and Barrel in Bradford, a modest pub with richly engraved window glass.

83 The restaurant at Whitelocks in Leeds. A traditional pub steeped in atmosphere, retaining its Victorian mirrors, brass fittings and stained glass.

84 Victorian bar in Beverley, faced in glazed tiles with a grand glass-fronted display case behind.

85 Yates Wine Lodge, Nottingham. The upstairs bar, complete with its traditional furnishings. Note the arched iron braces of the roof and the turned kingposts.

82

83

84

85

86

86 The Crown Hotel, Liverpool, with its gloriously
ornate plasterwork and lettering.

87 The Test Match Hotel near Trent Bridge. Dating
from 1938, it has one of the best preserved inter-war
pub interiors. Designed by A.C. Wheeler with fittings
by Harris & Sheldon.

87

88, **89** The bar in the Philharmonic, Liverpool's most famous pub. Dating from 1898, it is the work of Walter Thomas and craftsmen from the Liverpool School of Art.

'The pub is supposedly a national institution yet we have spent three decades demolishing pubs and refashioning those that remain.'

Kenneth Powell, **SAVE** report *Time Gentlemen Please!*

PALACE STREET

The local council bought long-empty
6 Palace Street, Caernarfon to restore it,
but then decided that it was beyond
repair and issued a dangerous structures
notice. Shortly before Christmas 1994
SAVE obtained engineering advice
showing how the building could be
stabilised. This was curtly rejected and the
Council said demolition would begin on 2
January. On New Year's Eve **SAVE**
obtained a Stay of Demolition in the High
Court, offering to put a 24-hour watch on
the building. Plans for repair were drawn
up by the architect Huw Thomas.

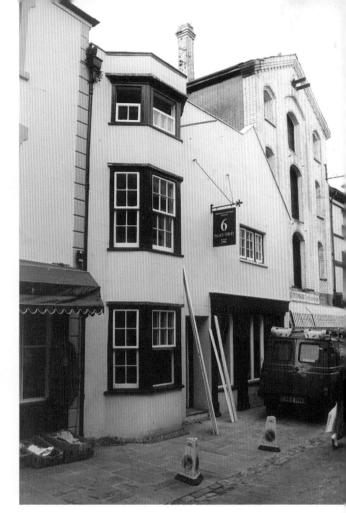

90

90 The street front with the restored triple-height bay
window.

91 Old photograph showing Palace Street.
Number 6 is on the right with the hanging sign.

92 The house shortly before acquisition by **SAVE**,
when the bay window had already been removed.

93

93, 94, 95 Inside 6 Palace Street, **SAVE**
uncovered the massive roof timbers of a 15th-century
first-floor hall.

94

95

BACK ON PARADE

Permission had been given for a highly damaging development scheme at Peninsula Barracks in Winchester, involving the demolition of half the historic buildings. With local architect Huw Thomas, **SAVE** obtained permission in 1994 for a new scheme that would open up the barracks to the town and convert all the historic buildings to residential use. Even at the depth of a property recession, **SAVE** found a property developer to carry out the scheme. A formal garden has been laid out over the bare tarmac, slightly raised to avoid damage to the archaeology beneath.

96

96 The disused parade ground at Peninsula Barracks, Winchester, in 1993. The grand barrack buildings on the right, designed by Ingress Bell, incorporate columns from the shell of Wren's Winchester Palace for Charles II, destroyed by fire on 19 December 1894.

97 The barracks, as restored.

98 Huw Thomas's initial sketch. At the far end of the parade ground, he proposed the reconstruction of the Italianate Officers' Terrace in place of a low 1960s block which was out of proportion with Ingress Bell's grand 'Wrennaissance' buildings.

97

98

99, 100 The barracks as completed to Huw Thomas's designs by Try Homes. Many of the handsome apartments and houses were sold to retired soldiers.

101 Peninsula Barracks, as envisaged by Huw Thomas in his residential conversion scheme for **SAVE**, published in **SAVE** report *Beauty or the Bulldozer*.

99

100

101

SAVING WREN'S CITY CHURCHES FROM CLOSURE

In 1994 the Templeman report published a list of 27 churches in the City of London which were candidates for closure, mothballing or secular use. The list included several of Sir Christopher Wren's finest churches, rebuilt after the Great Fire of London in 1666. **SAVE**'s report *The City Churches Have a Future* led directly to the establishment of the Friends of the City Churches, who now regularly provide volunteers enabling churches to be open to the public. Not one church has since been closed.

102 Wren's St Benet's, Paul's Wharf and, **103**, St Michael Cornhill: two of the churches threatened by the Templeman Commission.

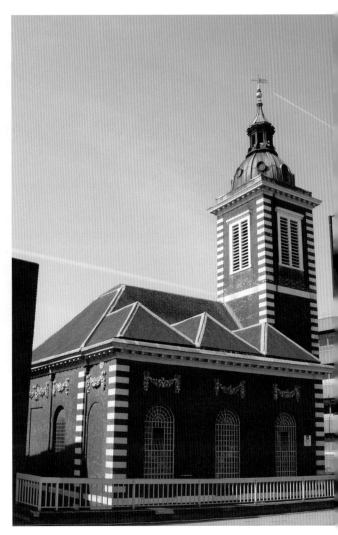

102

104 The tower of St Mary Aldermary and, **105** and **106**, the interior and spire of St Martin, Ludgate Hill: two Wren churches whose future was put into question by the Templeman Report. Today, however, they continue to be much visited and regularly used for worship.

104

105

106

ARE THEY INSANE?

Victorian mental asylums were built on sunny south facing sites, often with one acre of grounds to every ten patients. When the government announced that 100 out of 120 asylums were to be closed, the intention was to demolish the buildings and sell the sites for development. In 1995 **SAVE**'s pioneering report *Mind Over Matter* drew attention to the architectural importance and potential of these buildings, and over half have now been converted for residential or college use.

107, 108 Edwardian Severalls Hospital, near Colchester. Though **SAVE** has found a developer to carry out a scheme of conversion, the Department of Health continues to allow these handsome buildings to rot.

109 Victorian Wyfold Court in Oxfordshire was formerly used as a psychiatric hospital, but has now been attractively converted into apartments by the P. J. Livesey Group.

108

109

111

110

110, 111 St Francis, Haywards Heath, Sussex, successfully transformed into apartments.

112   113

112 Friern Barnet Hospital in north London, converted into apartments by Comer Homes.

113 The splendid Arts and Crafts Hospital at Carlton Hayes near Leicester, built in 1904 to the designs of S. P. Pick, an accomplished local architect, during demolition to make way for a car park for a new Alliance & Leicester Building Society headquarters.

'Not since the Beeching Axe fell on the railways has so large a slice of the nation's heritage been made so precipitately redundant.'

Mind over Matter

SAVE'S CONCRETE CASTLE

With repairs estimated at nearly £1m, this remarkable folly is one of the most formidable challenges **SAVE** has faced. Castle House in Bridgwater, Somerset, was built for William Akerman in 1851. It was both a family home and a showcase for the builder, John Board, who had invented Portland cement, a pioneering new building material. The **SAVE** Trust agreed to take on the long-empty building following compulsory purchase by the council. Now the Strummerville Trust, set up by friends of the musician Joe Strummer, plans to turn Castle House into the first of a series of centres bringing musical opportunities to young people in inner-city areas.

114

114 Concert to rally support for Castle House as a candidate in the BBC *Restoration* series. Pictured are Mick Jones (formerly of the Clash), Badly Drawn Boy, Andy Mackay from Roxy Music and actor Keith Allen.

115 The castle is a delightful dwelling, with a wealth of ornament and concrete blocks shaped to look like stone. The building is thought to be the earliest surviving example of the use of prefabricated concrete.

DANGER
BUILDING OPERATIONS
IN PROGRESS

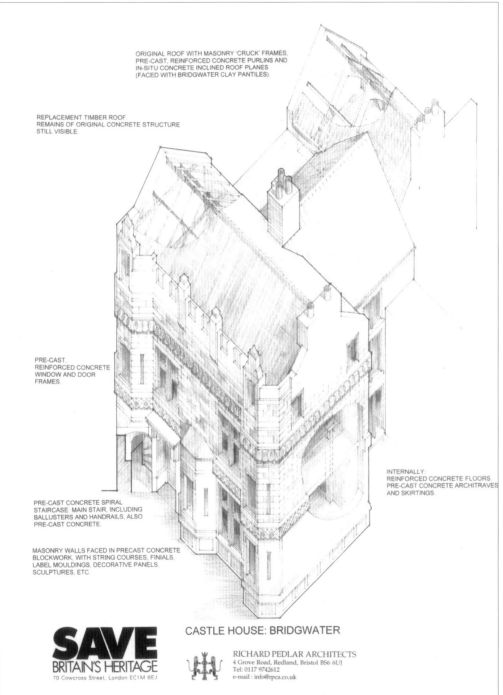

ORIGINAL ROOF WITH MASONRY 'CRUCK' FRAMES,
PRE-CAST, REINFORCED CONCRETE PURLINS AND
IN-SITU CONCRETE INCLINED ROOF PLANES
(FACED WITH BRIDGWATER CLAY PANTILES).

REPLACEMENT TIMBER ROOF.
REMAINS OF ORIGINAL CONCRETE STRUCTURE
STILL VISIBLE.

PRE-CAST,
REINFORCED CONCRETE
WINDOW AND DOOR
FRAMES.

INTERNALLY:
REINFORCED CONCRETE FLOORS.
PRE-CAST CONCRETE ARCHITRAVES
AND SKIRTINGS.

PRE-CAST CONCRETE SPIRAL
STAIRCASE: MAIN STAIR, INCLUDING
BALLUSTERS AND HANDRAILS, ALSO
PRE-CAST CONCRETE.

MASONRY WALLS FACED IN PRECAST CONCRETE
BLOCKWORK, WITH STRING COURSES, FINIALS,
LABEL MOULDINGS, DECORATIVE PANELS,
SCULPTURES, ETC.

CASTLE HOUSE: BRIDGWATER

SAVE
BRITAIN'S HERITAGE
70 Cowcross Street, London EC1M 6EJ

RICHARD PEDLAR ARCHITECTS
4 Grove Road, Redland, Bristol BS6 6UJ
Tel: 0117 9742612
e-mail : info@rpca.co.uk

117

116 An axonometric diagram of Castle House, showing the key components in its construction, which was at the forefront of technology for using precast concrete elements, post tensioning and a fascinating masonry 'cruck' structure for the roof.

117 Elaborate ornamental panel in pre-cast concrete damaged by structural movement and in urgent need of repair.

118

118 One of a number of handsome gargoyles specially cast for the house.

2000 - 2005

ENOUGH HAS BEEN BULLDOZED

Farnborough is the cradle of British aviation and spiritual home of flying in Britain. Yet only half a dozen buildings were listed. When the 108-acre site was sold for redevelopment, **SAVE** launched a campaign to retain the core historic area of 20 acres and drew up proposals to bring the former Royal Aircraft Establishment back to life as the central focus of a new office park, with a mix of uses and houses instead of offices on adjacent land. This strategy has now been adopted by the owners, Slough Estates.

119 Cover of **SAVE** report showing the 24–foot wind tunnel built in 1935, with 30–foot mahogany fan for sucking air over test models (and full-scale aircraft). It is a cathedral to flight, with its massive return air duct and air turning vanes constructed in concrete.

120 Test preparation in the 30–foot wind tunnel. Aircraft were suspended from the mechanical balance in the ceiling or supported by one under the test area. The complete survival of this machinery in all Farnborough's wind tunnels marks it out from other historic aviation sites, the world over.

ENOUGH HAS BEEN BULLDOZED!

SAVE FARNBOROUGH
THE CRADLE OF BRITISH AVIATION

119

120

R·A·E TRANSONIC TUNNELS

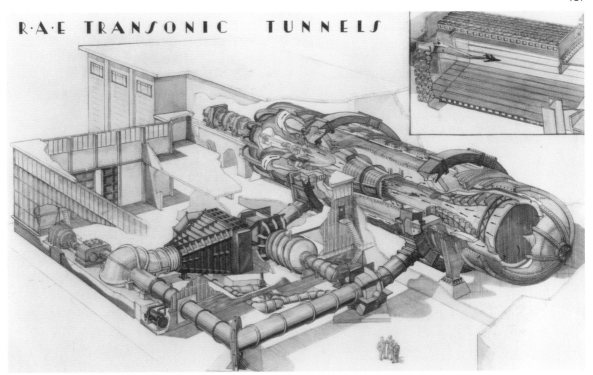

121 A diagram of the transonic wind tunnel. This remarkable piece of machinery was completed in 1942 and upgraded 1951 – 56. Essentially its function was to suck air over scale models of aircraft at transonic and supersonic speeds. Testing scale models required a commensurate increase in the air pressure, creating great heat through the friction of the air and therefore also requiring a mass of cooling equipment. Originally listed at Grade II, it is now listed at Grade I as a result of **SAVE**'s efforts.

122 Q121 is the nomenclature for the spectacular 24-foot wind tunnel at RAE Farnborough, completed in 1935. Its 30-foot mahogany fan can suck air over full-scale aircraft at a speed of up to 120mph. It makes use of a single return air duct, which reuses the air once it has passed over the aircraft by means of a series of beautifully formed turning vanes. Unlike any contemporary tunnel in the world, it has retained all its mechanical balances and other test equipment. **SAVE**'s work resulted in its protection being upgraded to Grade I.

'In 1908 Colonel Cody made the first powered flight in the UK from Farnborough and in 1911 the Royal Engineers Air Battalion, the forerunner of the RAF, was formed here.'

SAVE report *Enough Has Been Bulldozed*

123

124

123 The transonic wind tunnel was used to test the performance of high-speed aircraft including the supersonic interceptor, The Lightning. Operating at very high pressures, it required a mass of machinery to both power and cool it; the solution being an air duct resembling a giant thermos flask.

124 Scientists photographing a model of a delta-winged V-bomber in the working section of the transonic wind tunnel.

'Throughout the Cold War the Royal Aircraft Establishment served as
the main and enduring core of European aerodynamic knowledge.'

Andrew Nahum

ULSTER

125

125 Vernacular buildings in Northern Ireland have been especially vulnerable to the lack of enforcement in the listed buildings system. Of the 30,000 traditional thatched cottages standing in the 1950s, only 120 remain intact. The Second Survey of buildings of architectural and historic interest has led to further delistings – with the building being punished rather than the owner for neglect.

126 Gosford Castle is owned by the Northern Ireland Forestry Service. It is currently abandoned and subject to minimal maintenance. The government in Northern Ireland is failing the public interest by not declaring its hand with this magnificent building – rather it appears to be leaving it to rot.

127 Tillie and Henderson Shirt Factory, Derry. The Secretary of State refused to either stop the demolition or prosecute the Grade B+ listed building's owner, claiming that to have taken measures to secure the building would have had an unacceptable effect on traffic flow in the city.

126

127

THE TYNTESFIELD EMERGENCY

This grand but little-known house in North Somerset had some of the most colourful and richly decorated Victorian interiors still surviving with their original furnishings. When the late Lord Wraxall left a will dividing his inheritance between 19 heirs, break-up seemed inevitable. **SAVE**'s campaign in 2002 played a crucial part in persuading the National Heritage Memorial Fund to provide a grant of £17.4m to enable the National Trust to acquire the house complete.

128 The staircase hall with a glimpse of the carved doorway to the dining room.

128

129

130

'I feel quite confident in saying that there is now no other Victorian country house which so richly represents its age as Tyntesfield – perhaps Cragside comes closest but its contents do not approach those of Tyntesfield in abundance and overall quality.'

Mark Girouard, 2002

131

129 The garden front. The facades are ornamented with exquisitely carved sculptural detail.

130 Late 19th-century photograph of the chapel at Tyntesfield, added 1873 – 75 to the designs of Sir Arthur Blomfield. The fittings are of the very highest quality, including the screen and gates at the entrance to the chancel by Barkentin & Krall.

131 Late 19th-century photograph of Tyntesfield, built 1863 – 66 to the designs of John Norton. The entrance tower and the large conservatory behind the house have been demolished.

LAW COURTS

SAVE's 2004 report *Silence in Court*, which published numerous never before seen handsome court room interiors, is the first fully illustrated study of court architecture. Splendid court houses in Carlisle, Derby, Devizes, and Liverpool have already closed but deserve to be preserved with their fine fittings intact. **SAVE** supported local people in a successful fight to prevent the closure of Knutsford. The choice of the Art Nouveau Gothic Middlesex Guildhall as the seat of the proposed new Supreme Court poses a threat to a series of magnificent interiors recently restored and in active court use.

132

132 The handsome Regency Court at Knutsford, Cheshire. **SAVE** fought a campaign alongside the local politicians, journalists and bench to prevent the closure of George Moneypenny's 1817 – 19 Sessions House, following the collapse of some of the decorative plasterwork in one of the courts – years of neglect finally taking their toll.

133 The Shire Hall in Derby, dating from 1659, is the earliest surviving purpose-built Assize court in England. The main threat to historic court buildings is at present the Public Private Partnership, which makes it cheaper for court operators to run large single facilities rather than a number of small, local courts. The extension of Derbyshire Hall under the Private Finance Initiative resulted in a poor-quality new building being erected on the site of the Georgian Judges' lodgings.

134

134 The continuity of the seats of justice is remarkable: Leicester Castle housed courts of one kind or another from 1273 through to the 1990s. The building is empty and unused. The local authority, which owns the building, now has the added burden of finding a future for this wonderful place, with fine furniture and fittings designed for a very specific use.

135 One of the finest Neo-Classical buildings in the world, Harvey Lonsdale Elms' splendid courthouse closed in 1984 and remained empty and decaying for over a decade – the Lord Chancellor's department having previously paid 97% of the running costs. The council formed a trust to raise the money to repair the building for all kinds of events, with the help of grants from the Heritage Lottery Fund.

DON'T BUTCHER SMITHFIELD

Indoor and outdoor markets add life and colour to any city. **SAVE** is fighting the proposed demolition of the old General Market and Fish Market at the west end of Smithfield, which developers want to replace with a 10-storey office block. Eric Reynolds, the man behind the successful regeneration of Camden Lock and Spitalfields Market, has put forward proposals for reusing the General Market on lines similar to the now flourishing Borough Market in Southwark.

136 The boy on a dolphin over Horace Jones's threatened Fish Market at Smithfield.

137 **SAVE** campaign poster for Smithfield. The general market buildings by Sir Horace Jones, completed in 1888. An application has just been submitted for consent to demolish the General Market on the left with the distinctive canopy linking the General Market with the Fish Market on the right.

DON'T BUTCHER SMITHFIELD

The Corporation of London wants to demolish the Smithfield General Market buildings between Farringdon Road, Snow Hill and West Poultry Avenue and replace them with a nine storey 780,000 sq ft major office development (seen right looking south).

THE GENERAL MARKET BUILDINGS ARE AN IMPORTANT PART OF THE WHOLE SMITHFIELD AREA AND THEY SHOULD BE REVITALISED AND REUSED.

PROTEST!

WRITE TO THE CITY PLANNING OFFICER, GUILDHALL, LONDON EC2P 2EJ.

For more information and to register opposition please contact SAVE Britain's Heritage
smithfield@savebritheritage.plus.com
70 Cowcross Street
London EC1M 6EJ
tel 020 7253 3500

registered charity no 269129

SAVE
BRITAIN'S HERITAGE

BULLDOZING THE NORTH

Up to 100,000 traditional terrace houses are under threat of demolition in the north-west of England. Many are still lived in and have been proudly restored by residents who desperately wish to remain. Often the houses have been condemned on the basis of no more than a cursory inspection. These photographs, commissioned by **SAVE**, show condemned streets and neighbour-hoods where houses are well maintained, brightly painted and far from derelict.

138

138 Terraced housing in the Bradley Ward of Nelson. Having successfully fought off a major clearance plan in Whitefield, Nelson, the bulldozer might well next be looking at Bradley Ward, where the pattern of terraced housing and mill is still legible.

139 The proposed clearances in Liverpool are particularly vicious, with a planned 10,000 demolitions, in spite of a waiting list of 20,000 for housing. The clearance areas are dominated by registered social landlords, which have purposely run down the areas in order to clear them and benefit from their development value – they are often close to public amenities and have good transport links.

139

140

141

142

140 Substantial three-storey terraced housing in Liverpool threatened with demolition. The community in this area has effectively been destroyed by the blight of knowing that their area might be threatened with clearance – and replacement with a city academy. 'Ten-minute condition surveys' of the houses, commissioned by the local authority, found the majority to be in poor condition and in need of demolition. More detailed surveys by professionals found exactly the opposite to be true.

141 Preemptive demolition in Bootle. Houses owned by a registered social landlord in Bootle have been cleared, leaving only three houses in the street standing – one either side of a house that is privately owned. Such intimidatory tactics are being employed to force the clearance of areas.

142 A pair of semi-detatched houses along the Edge Lane in Liverpool, threatened with clearance as part of a road widening scheme. They are deemed 'unsuitable for modern living' by the agencies charged with their demolition: English Partnerships, Liverpool City Council and the Housing Market Renewal body 'New Heartlands', rapidly dubbed by Liverpudlians as 'New Heartbreak' and 'New Wastelands'.

PADDINGTON STATION SPAN FOUR

The roofs of grand city termini have always been one of the great glories of railway architecture – perhaps the greatest glory. When Brunel's original terminus at Paddington needed enlarging the railway engineer W. Y. Armstrong added an imposing fourth arched roof, carefully matching Brunel's original design of a central nave and two aisles. The proportions of Span 4 are extraordinarily well-judged; indeed they are large enough for the arched roof to hold its own, but in no way do they overwhelm the original.

143

143, 144, 145 Span 4 of Paddington Station is currently threatened with demolition and replacement with an office block. Built by the Great Western Railway under the auspices of W. Y. Armstrong, its chief engineer, and completed in 1916, it represents both the Great Western Railway at its apogee and a sensitive, yet spectacular addition to Brunel's masterpiece. It has been hidden from public view by an ugly crash deck for the last decade.

146 Eric de Mare's iconic view of Armstrong's roof.

145

146

SAVED

HUNDREDS OF COUNTRY HOUSES, CHURCHES AND CHAPELS, NUMEROUS

IMPOSING WAREHOUSES AND TEXTILE MILLS AND HISTORIC STRUCTURES OF

ALMOST EVERY TYPE HAVE BEEN REPRIEVED AND GIVEN A NEW LEASE OF LIFE

AS A RESULT OF **SAVE**'S EFFORTS AND PUBLICITY. **SAVE**'S APPROACH IS

TWOFOLD: FIRST, TO HELP VIGOROUSLY AT THE TIME OF GREATEST THREAT;

AND SECOND, TO TAKE A LEAD IN PROPOSING POSITIVE AND VIABLE NEW

SOLUTIONS FOR REPAIR AND REUSE.

CULLEN HOUSE

147

147 Cullen House, Banffshire. **SAVE** led opposition to the demolition of this magnificent baronial house. Standing empty and suffering from extensive dry rot, it was acquired in 1981 by Kit Martin and restored as a series of substantial houses with smaller cottages in the office court. Dating from 1600, the house was spectacularly remodelled from 1869 onwards by David Bryce, the foremost exponent of the Scottish Baronial style.

HOUSE OF GRAY

148

148 The House of Gray, with its delightful bell-topped towers, was built in 1716 for the 12th Lord Gray and is attributed to the architect Alexander McGill. After more years of neglect the house has now been externally repaired and given a new coat of lime mortar, following the evidence of an early 19th- century painting.

149

149, 150 When **SAVE** first took up the cause of the House of Gray near Dundee the house had not been lived in since 1938. The slates had been torn from the roof. Floors and ceilings had disappeared. The gutters had gone and rain was cascading down the handsome stone facades washing away the fine carved detail of swags and coats of arms.

150

HYLANDS HOUSE

151

152

151, 152 Hylands House and its splendid Repton landscape was bought by Chelmsford Council in 1966 to create a public park outside the town, but the house was left to decay and in 1975, European Architectural Heritage Year, councillors voted for demolition. **SAVE** led the opposition and consent was rejected following a public inquiry. The house was remodelled in grand Regency style for a Danish merchant Cornelius Kortwright who owned large estates in the West Indies. Now the house has been restored by Chelmsford Council. It is open to the public two days a week and is let for weddings and events on other days.

153

153 Ecton Hall, Northamptonshire. This enchanting mid-18th century house in Strawberry Hill Gothick style is attributed to the Hiorn brothers of Warwick. Despite sustained publicity in **SAVE** reports it was left empty and decaying and the Council refused to serve a repairs notice. When finally offered for sale it was quickly bought and converted into apartments.

SHAW HOUSE NEWBURY

154

154 Shaw House, on the edge of Newbury, is a grand Elizabethan house completed in 1581 for the clothier Thomas Dolman. It had been taken over as a girls' school when discovery of dry rot prompted the school to vacate the house and strip out much of the fine panelling. At one time the formal garden was threatened with development to raise funds but in 2005 a £4m Heritage Lottery Grant enabled West Berkshire Council to begin restoration of the house for education and community use.

AXWELL PARK GATESHEAD

155

155, 156 Axwell Park, County Durham, was built in 1758 for Sir Thomas Clavering, to the designs of James Paine. After serving as a borstal it was left and heavily vandalised. It has recently been acquired by the DARE Group and will be restored as apartments. Ugly modern accretions will be removed and the landscape around the house restored.

156

CHILLINGHAM CASTLE

157

157 Chillingham Castle, Northumberland is a
quadrangular fortified house dating largely from the
mid—14th century with a splendid classical 1630s
frontispiece. When published in **SAVE**'s report
Tomorrow's Ruins in 1977 it stood empty and
abandoned. Soon after the castle was acquired by
Sir Humphrey Wakefield, who rescued the castle from
decay and opens it regularly to the public and hosts
a constant stream of banquets, weddings and events.

PECKFORTON CASTLE

158

158 Peckforton Castle, Cheshire was built in the
1840s to the designs of Anthony Salvin for the 1st Lord
Tollemache, with masonry as massive as any medieval
castle. **SAVE** highlighted its plight when leaking roofs
had begun to seriously damage the stonework. It is
now a hotel.

BURLEY-ON-THE-HILL

159

159, 160 Burley-on-the-Hill had been acquired for hotel use in the 1980s when controversial additions were planned. When these proposals fell through following strong opposition from **SAVE** it was bought by Kit Martin and restored as 23 self-contained houses, six in the main block and others in the wings. The house was built for the 2nd Earl of Nottingham in the late 1690s.

HIGHCLIFFE CASTLE

161 Highcliffe Castle, Dorset was begun in the 1830s by Lord Stuart de Rothesay, a former Ambassador to France, who incorporated fragments of French Gothic buildings in his house. After two serious fires the building stood a gutted shell surrounded by barbed wire in a public park. A long campaign finally persuaded Christchurch Council to withdraw plans for demolition and restore the house, which is now open to the public and used for events.

161

MIDDLETON HALL WARWICKS

162, 163 Middleton Hall, Warwickshire was falling into ruin when first illustrated by **SAVE**. Since then it has been rescued from ruin by the Middleton Hall trust. The long Georgian wing and the 16th-century Great Hall have been restored and the house is now regularly used for weddings.

TODDINGTON MANOR

164, 165 Toddington Manor, Gloucestershire, designed and built for himself 1819 – 35 by Charles Hanbury-Tracy, chairman of the commission appointed to judge the designs for the new Houses of Parliament. **SAVE** fought proposals to add a 200-bedroom wing to the house. It has now been acquired by Damien Hirst, who will restore it and use it to display his collection.

164

165

MARSTON HALL

166, 167 Marston Hall, Somerset, built by the
Earls of Cork and Orrery in the early 18th century and
remodelled in 1751 and 1776. One of many empty and
endangered country houses featured in early **SAVE**
reports, it has been handsomely restored as the
headquarters of Foster Yeoman Ltd.

167

166

THREE GRACES

169

168, 169 Canova's *Three Graces*. Canova's famous statue was acquired by the National Galleries of Scotland and the V&A after a long battle to prevent its export. **SAVE** played a key role in the early stages of this battle, contending that the statue was protected by listing as it stood in a temple designed by Sir Jeffry Wyatville specially to display it. This case went to the High Court where Government lawyers undertook to rule on the matter. Though they ruled against **SAVE**, the delaying action gained time for others to successfully take on the battle.

LIGHTCLIFFE UNITED REFORMED CHURCH

170

170 This impressive Victorian Congregational Church in the leafy suburb of Lightcliffe near Halifax was one of **SAVE**'s first cases. Built in 1871 to the designs of leading Bradford architects Lockwood and Mawson, and cleaned and redecorated for its centenary, it was threatened soon after by replacement with a block of flats. In 1982 it reopened as a craft centre.

ST JOHN'S READING

171

171, 172 St John's Reading. A handsome local landmark built in 1872 – 74 to the designs of W.A. Dixon in muscular French Gothic style. Demolition had been approved but **SAVE** campaigned for a reprieve, arguing that the church would make an excellent home for the large local Polish Roman Catholic community, who had no church of their own. Demolition was halted when Reading Council refused the Church Commissioners permission to demolish the listed wall along the road to allow access for bulldozers. In 1981 the Poles moved in with a grand celebratory mass.

172

ST FRANCIS XAVIER

173

173 St Francis Xavier, Liverpool, built 1845 – 49 to the designs of the leading Catholic architect John Joseph Scoles. Plans were announced to demolish this magnificent listed Catholic church, leaving only the tower and lady chapel. Exemption from listed building consent was claimed on the grounds that the building was in ecclesiastical use. **SAVE** mounted a legal challenge, arguing that the church could not be in ecclesiastical use if the major part was being demolished. The church authorities relented and have carried out an exemplary restoration.

HOLY TRINITY PRIVETT

174

174 Holy Trinity Church in Privett, Hampshire is a sumptuous Victorian interior with fittings of the highest quality. When it was closed in the 1970s proposals were put forward for converting it into a house. **SAVE** argued it should be preserved intact and the church is now cared for by the Churches Conservation Trust.

HEADINGLEY HILL UNITED REFORMED CHURCH

175

175 Headingley Hill United Reformed Church in
Leeds was built in the 1860s to designs of Cuthbert
Brodrick, the architect of Leeds's magnificent town hall.
Conversion to offices by the Bulldog Design Partnership
has kept it as a single grand open space rising to the
roof timbers.

CHRISTIAN SCIENCE CHURCH MANCHESTER

176

176 The Christian Scientist Church in Manchester's Victoria Park was built in Arts and Crafts style by the architect Edgar Wood. In a model conversion it has become a performing arts centre for a nearby education college.

SQUARE CHAPEL HALIFAX

177

178

177, 178 The handsome Square Chapel in Halifax, dating from 1772, was one of the most handsome of all Georgian Dissenters' chapels. Though owned by the local authority it was allowed to become a near-ruin in the early 1980s, but has now been restored as an arts centre with a packed programme of music, dance and community events.

CHURCH OF THE HOLY NAME MANCHESTER

179

179 The Catholic Church of the Holy Name
Manchester, completed in 1871, was designed for
the Jesuits by Joseph Aloysius Hansom, inventor of the
Hansom cab. It came under sudden threat when the
Jesuits decided to leave. **SAVE** strongly supported a
local campaign for its retention and it is now one of the
best attended churches in the city.

CLIFTON UNITED REFORMED CHURCH

180, 181 Clifton United Reformed Church, Bristol, by Charles Hansom, 1868. Built in a spiky French style with a beautifully vaulted triple-arched porch. A legal challenge by **SAVE** solicitor David Cooper halted the imminent demolition of this prominent local landmark. It was then successfully converted into flats by Bob Trapnell and Domus Design and Build in 1987.

UNION CHAPEL ISLINGTON

183

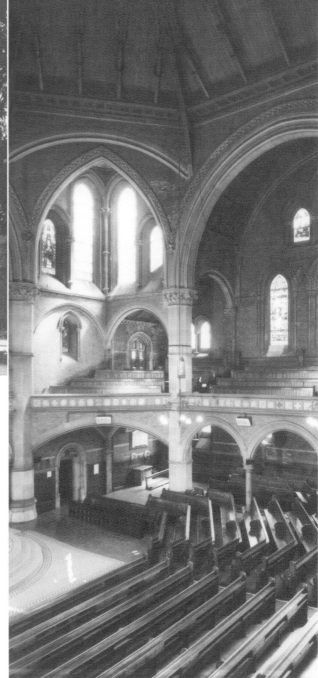

182

182, 183 Union Chapel, Islington, London. This towering landmark was counted as one of the ten best surviving town chapels by Christopher Stell, leading historian of Chapel architecture. Sadly, as the congregation had dwindled and repairs were estimated at £500,000, demolition was proposed. The **SAVE** Union Chapel report was published in October 1981 just as Islington Borough Council had agreed to demolition. A reprieve was secured, architect Tony Richardson advised the congregation on a phased programme of repairs, grants were secured and the imposing galleried interior is now let for numerous events.

BETHESDA

184

184, 185, 186, 187 Bethesda Chapel, Hanley,
Stoke-on-Trent, built for a congregation of up to 3,000,
dates from 1820 but has a handsome Italianate front
added in 1859. As the congregation shrank, consent
to demolish was sought in 1982 but, after a sustained
battle, the chapel was taken on by the Historic Chapels
Trust and will now be restored.

185

187

186

DERBY RAILWAY VILLAGE

188

188 Derby Railway Village, built in the early 1840s.
This delightful triangle of railway workers' cottages
was badly decayed and threatened with demolition.
SAVE ran a press campaign in support of local objectors
and the houses were taken on and restored by the
Derbyshire Historic Buildings Trust.

CRESSBROOK MILL

189

189 Serenely elegant Cressbrook Mill was built 1814 – 16 and stands in the Peak District National Park in Derbyshire. After production ceased in the 1960s it fell steadily into decay. **SAVE**'s 1990 report *Bright Futures* included plans by the architect Francis Machin for restoring the mill as 13 houses and ten apartments. Repair and conversion has been undertaken by the mill's owners and almost all the apartments have been sold.

THE CANTERBURY TANNERY

190, 191, 192 The Tannery in Canterbury stands just inside the city walls, straddling the River Stour. When plans were submitted to redevelop the site which is in a conservation area, **SAVE** commissioned a scheme showing how the historic buildings could be preserved and converted; an approach which has now been adopted by the developer.

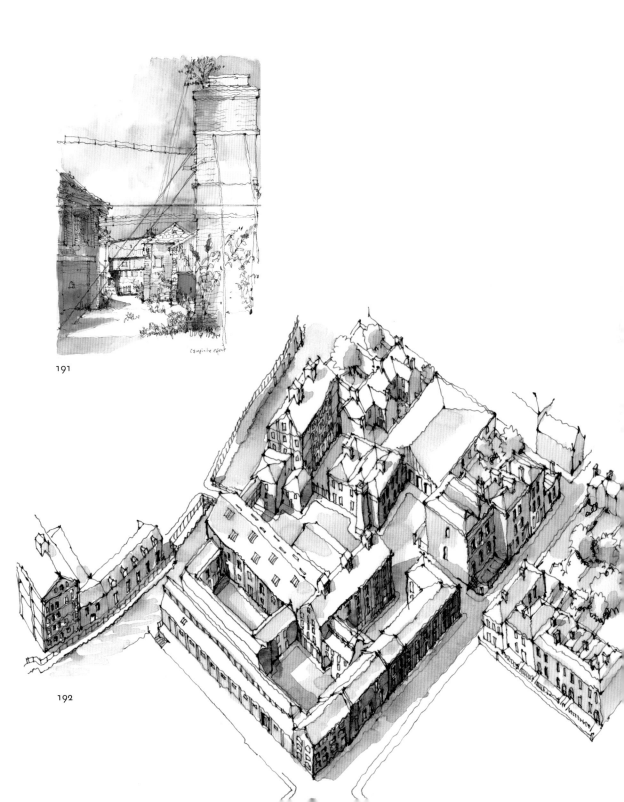

191

192

TEMPLE MEADS BRISTOL

193

193 Old Temple Meads Station, Brunel's original
Great Western Railway terminus in Bristol, was in a
serious state of decay when included in **SAVE**'s 1977
exhibition *Off the Rails*. Soon after, it was taken on
by an independent trust, which raised over £1m for
repairs. It now houses the much-visited Museum of
Empire. Recent cleaning of Brunel's handsome
stonework has been supported by grants from the
Railway Heritage Trust.

BERWICK-ON-TWEED

194

194 **SAVE** gave strong support to a local campaign opposing the building of 50 retirement apartments in the gardens of the former Governor's Palace at Berwick-on-Tweed. The new building would have loomed above Berwick's magnificent ramparts, the finest in the country. The plans were rejected following a public inquiry.

RODBORO BUILDINGS GUILDFORD

195 Rodboro Building, Guildford . One of the earliest car factories in Britain, built in 1901 by John Dennis, who went on to build thousands of army lorries in the First World War. A **SAVE** campaign helped avert demolition. Restored and reused, it is now a public house and a prominent local landmark.

BOATHOUSE 4

196, 197 Number 4 Boathouse, Portsmouth was begun in 1938 as part of the rapid rearmament programme before World War II. Though it was not listed, **SAVE** secured a reprieve from demolition, arguing that its lofty interior could provide a valuable flexible space for exhibitions and events in Portsmouth's historic dockyard. Architect Huw Thomas suggested that the corrugated iron covering the unfinished end could be replaced by glass with a display of boats and planes inside.

196

197

CATERHAM BARRACKS

198

199

198, 199 The Guards' Barracks at Caterham, Surrey were due to be sold and entirely demolished for housing redevelopment. **SAVE** argued that the imposing series of barrack blocks, overlooking a cricket ground, could be converted as apartments. The proposal was adopted by the purchasers of the site Linden Homes and cleaning has revealed handsome polychrome brickwork.

SHOEBURYNESS GARRISON

200

200 Shoeburyness Barracks were included in **SAVE**'s 1993 exhibition *Deserted Bastions*. As **SAVE** proposed, all the handsome Regency and Victorian buildings have been successfully converted and sold.

LIVERPOOL LYCEUM

201

201 The Lyceum, Liverpool. Permission had been granted for demolition of this Greek Revival master-piece, built to the designs of Thomas Harrison of Chester, 1800 – 03. In 1978 a sustained campaign by **SAVE** and numerous local objectors persuaded ministers to intervene and revoke the planning permission. Here it is shown in use as a Post Office.

SUN STREET

202

203

202, 203 Sun Street, Islington, London. **SAVE** strongly opposed the demolition of this row of run-down but dignified Georgian houses, which make an attractive composition with the Victorian pub on the corner. With the support of the Spitalfields Trust, which has restored many derelict houses nearby, **SAVE** argued that the houses could be incorporated within a new development on adjacent land; a proposal adopted by the developers.

BILLINGSGATE

204

205

204, 205 Old Billingsgate Fish Market, built to the designs of the City architect Sir Horace Jones, 1874 – 78. The City Corporation intended to demolish this handsome landmark on the Thames to recoup the £7.4m of moving the fish market to docklands. **SAVE** approached Lord Rogers to prepare plans for reusing the market (drawn up by architects Ian Ritchie and Alan Stanton). After Michael Heseltine spotlisted the building in 1980, the site was sold on the basis of the **SAVE** scheme for £22m. The market was restored by the Richard Rogers Partnership and is now in continuous demand for events.

'Although the present Billingsgate Market is less than a hundred years old, the corrosive effects of fish juice mean it has to be rebuilt.''

The Corporation's Year, 1979

REGENT PALACE HOTEL

206

206, 207, 208 Oliver Bernard's fabulous Art Deco interiors survive intact in the basement of the Regent Palace Hotel at Piccadilly Circus in London. A wealth of other details survive throughout this massive hotel, which has been providing affordable rooms at the heart of the city for nearly a century. Its owners, the Crown Estate, wanted to demolish the building and replace it with an office block. These plans were fought off following the listing of the building and presentations to Westminster City Council's planning committee.

207

208

AT RISK NOW

OVER 30 YEARS, **SAVE** HAS ILLUSTRATED HUNDREDS OF EMPTY AND

DECAYING HISTORIC BUILDINGS IN ITS REPORTS AND PRESS RELEASES. OF

THESE, MANY HAVE FOUND NEW OWNERS OR NEW USES, BUT CURRENTLY

SOME 900 **BUILDINGS AT RISK** ARE DESCRIBED AND ILLUSTRATED ON

OUR WEBSITE. HERE FOLLOWS A SMALL SELECTION OF FINE BUILDINGS

GWRYCH CASTLE

209

209, 210, 211, 212, 213, 214, 215 Gwrych
Castle, north Wales, begun in 1819 by Lloyd Hesketh
Bamford-Hesketh. He was largely his own architect,
though he employed Thomas Rickman, a pioneer of
cast-iron tracery for Gothic buildings, as an advisor.
The castle was sold in 1946 to Mr Leslie Salts, who
opened it to the public for 20 years, attracting nearly
ten million visitors and earning Gwrych the sobriquet of
'the showplace of Wales'. In 1989 the castle was sold
to a property developer in California and during 16
years of absentee ownership the roofs have collapsed
bringing down ceilings and floors. The castle is due to
be sold by auction in December 2005. A building
preservation trust is seeking to preserve it.

210   211

212

213

214

215

KINMEL HALL

216

216 Kinmel Hall, Denbighshire, built 1871 – 74 by W. E. Nesfield for H. R. Hughes, whose family fortune was founded on copper. One of the grandest houses ever built by a 'commoner', it is designed in the style of Wren, as manifest in his work on Hampton Court Palace. Restored as an evangelical conference centre after a fire, it now desperately needs a new use.

GUY'S CLIFFE

217

218

217, 218 Guy's Cliffe, Warwickshire. The entire fittings were auctioned in 1952 and the lead stripped after permission for a housing estate was refused. The Palladian house, from which the actress Sarah Siddons eloped in 1773, was built by Samuel Greatheed in the 1750s and given a new Gothic front by his son Bertie 1819 – 24. The chapel is used by local Masonic groups but the house remains a shell. The shell has been stabilised after permission to demolish was refused and is a prime candidate for reconstruction for residential use.

HIGHHEAD CASTLE

219

219, 220 Highhead Castle, Cumberland. This
glorious 1740s house, based on designs by James
Gibbs, was built for a young man in his twenties, Henry
Richmond Brougham. Featured in early **SAVE** reports, it
has been saved from demolition by Christopher Terry
but funds are critically required before a full restoration
can be undertaken.

RENAULT SWINDON

221

221 The Renault factory in Swindon by Foster & Partners, built as a distribution centre in 1983. Empty since 1999 and now in urgent demand of a new function.

MECHANICS INSTITUTE SWINDON

222

222, 223 Mechanics' Institute, Swindon, built 1955, enlarged 1892. It was long abandoned and vandalised, but now a new owner has begun to scaffold the building with a view to converting it into flats.

223

COLLIER STREET BATHS

225

224, 225 Collier Street Baths, Salford, Lancashire. One of the earliest surviving municipal bathhouses in Britain. They opened in 1856 with first and second class vapour and slipper baths. Now empty and under threat.

LOST BUILDINGS IN THE HEART OF THE CITY OF LONDON

Jennifer Freeman

At the end of the 40-year Mansion House/Poultry redevelopment saga in 1997 a new office building designed by James Stirling stood at Bank junction, opposite the Royal Exchange with the Bank of England to the north.

Twenty-four historic buildings, eight of them listed, occupying four triangular blocks, had been erased. All of these buildings were once sited in the designated Bank conservation area. Most were Victorian or Edwardian mercantile and commercial buildings with at least one 1920s building of distinction and a rare surviving Georgian house. A network of medieval lanes had disappeared. Probably the last surviving Roman City street – Bucklersbury – had been obliterated. Two historic church sites and burial grounds had vanished. Two interesting Victorian pubs and a host of small shops and offices had been excised, including the landmark Mappin & Webb corner building. The battle to save this fascinating enclave had been hard fought but ultimately lost.

The present Lord Palumbo's father had begun assembling the site in 1958. As leases fell in, buildings were emptied. Businesses departed. Some buildings in the area were gutted in the 1970s.

The first redevelopment proposal – for a new square and skyscraper tower – designed by architect Mies van der Rohe in the 1960s, was refused planning permission and listed building consent in 1985 after a celebrated two-month public enquiry. A huge number of bodies, including **SAVE**, gave evidence for and against the development plans. In refusing planning permission, the Secretary of State, Patrick Jenkin, opened the door for another chance to produce 'an acceptable scheme'.

Seizing the opportunity, Palumbo employed James Stirling to design the present office building, which covers the whole appeal site and incorporates shops, a new access to Bank Tube Station, a roof garden and penthouse restaurant.

The proposals were fought by **SAVE**, accompanied by a large group of public and private amenity bodies, both local and national, including English Heritage which produced an alternative refurbishment scheme (leading on from an earlier Terry Farrell scheme proposed by **SAVE** at the Mansion House Inquiry). Despite these endeavours, the Stirling scheme won acceptance after this second public inquiry in 1988.

SAVE was dissatisfied with the outcome of the Poultry Inquiry and questioned the inspector's reliance on a subjective comparison of the Stirling design and the existing historic buildings. 'It might just be a masterpiece,' he announced, giving little weight to the 'presumption' in favour of the retention of listed buildings in official planning guidelines.

226 The Mappin & Webb triangle forming a delightful Gothic contrast to the grand classical portico of the Mansion House.

227 Crisp, lively detail on an entrance archway.

228 A Victorian shopfront complete with cast-iron columns and original lettering in the frieze above.

229, 230 Mappin & Webb, with its distinctive circular tower, formed a delightful Gothic contrast to the august portico of London's Mansion House. It was one of a series of unusual triangular buildings of great variety and character built when Queen Victoria Street was laid out in the 1870s, cutting diagonally through the street pattern.

229

SAVE took legal action, losing in the High Court, winning in the Court of Appeal and finally losing in the House of Lords, where, most unfairly in the view of many, costs of £90,000 were awarded against **SAVE**, even though the Government had been happy not to pursue the matter after the Appeal Court decision.

A third public inquiry followed over the road closures required to implement the Stirling scheme. This inquiry was lost also, though changes had to be made at ground level to improve pedestrian circulation. Thus Lord Palumbo was free to implement his redevelopment scheme in partnership with Dieter Bock, a German financier and developer. After 40 years of blight, the new office building was finally completed and opened in 1997.

An archaeological excavation carried out at the time revealed extensive remains of Roman and later London. The turret from the top of the Mappin & Webb building ended up in the garden of Lord Palumbo's Mies house in the United States! It was always possible to refurbish the historic buildings on the site, but they were wantonly destroyed.

230

WHAT PEOPLE SAID ABOUT THE
MANSION HOUSE SQUARE PROPOSAL

'A giant glass stump better suited to Chicago' *(HRH Prince of Wales)*

'The wrong building in the wrong place at the wrong time' *(John Harris)*

WHAT PEOPLE SAID ABOUT THE STIRLING SCHEME

'A 1930s wireless set' *(HRH Prince of Wales)*

'It is still hopelessly inappropriate in the local context … perhaps the most significant aspect of the scheme is its obliteration of the view of St Paul's from Cornhill' *(Roy Worskett)*

'I find that from the viewpoint of pedestrian comfort and safety, the proposed development would have some serious design defects. It would certainly be less than a masterpiece; it might just be disastrous' *(G. F. Self, Inspector, Road Closures Public Inquiry)*

'And now this large bully has arrived, decidedly in your face. It contrives to be both solid and flashy, like a rogue City trader' *(Colin Amery)*

'It is a sad day for heritage and for the art of architecture when modern architects have to destroy the good work of the predecessors. We still believe the alternative design we proposed would have provided adequate and viable modern office space while respecting famous and well loved Victorian buildings on the site' *(Lord Montagu of Beaulieu, Chairman, English Heritage)*

WHAT PEOPLE SAID ABOUT THE LOST BUILDINGS

'If anyone is to feel nostalgic about the existing buildings on No. 1 Poultry, it is surely I! I have known them intimately over half my life and in all conscience, it is time they went. They will. I do not think the brain dead should linger interminably' *(Lord Palumbo)*

'J & J Belcher's joyfully Gothic Mappin & Webb building, marching in among the great classical monuments at the head of an army of variously dressed Victorian mercenaries, points up the scale and grandeur of the public buildings, lending historical depth to their content in a way that is the quintessence of the City's traditional architectural character.

(John Maddison, Victorian Society)

ACKNOWLEDGEMENTS

This book is published as a companion to the **SAVE** exhibition at the RIBA Architecture Gallery at the Victoria and Albert Museum. Our thanks are due first to Charles Hind and Michael Snodin, who suggested the exhibition, and to Susan Pugh, Assistant Curator at the RIBA Drawings and Archives Collections of the V&A. The exhibition was designed by Robin Ollington. The digital scanning and photographic printing has been done by James Mortimer to a very high standard, which has been enormously helpful in the production of this book.

Adam Wilkinson, **SAVE**'s Secretary, has provided assistance at every stage of the book. Further help has come from Ela Palmer and Dale Ingram at **SAVE**.

This book provides a wonderful opportunity to illustrate some of the superb photographs taken for **SAVE** over 30 years, notably by Christopher Dalton, Mark Fiennes, Keith Parkinson and Ian Beesley. We are very grateful to be able to reproduce excellent photographs supplied for earlier **SAVE** reports by the National Monuments Record and the National Monuments Record for Scotland, as well as key photographs by John Donat and Alex Starkey. Sophie Andreae, Richard Pollard, Matthew Saunders and Oliver Leigh-Wood have helped in checking important points. Jennifer Freeman has kindly written the Envoi on the Mappin & Webb triangle.

Neither book nor exhibition would have been possible without the generous sponsorship of the DARE Group.

SAVE has produced many lightning reports but none as ambitious as this. The idea for the book was agreed with David Campbell of Scala on 6 October 2005. Oliver Craske and Sarah Peacock at Scala have worked at intense speed to edit the book, Misha Anikst and Alfonso Iacurci have completed the design and page layouts and scanned all the illustrations within three weeks, and Tim Clarke has pulled out all the stops to get the books printed and delivered.